REFERENCE GUIDES IN LITERATURE

Everett Emerson, *Editor*

Roger Williams
A Reference Guide

Wallace Coyle

G. K. HALL & CO., 70 LINCOLN STREET, BOSTON, MASS.

Copyright © 1977 by Wallace Coyle

Library of Congress Cataloging in Publication Data

Coyle, Wallace.
   Roger Williams : a reference guide.

   (Reference guides in literature)
   Includes indexes.
   1. Williams, Roger, 1604?-1683--Bibliography.
Z8976.42.C68   [F82.W]   016.9745'02'0924   76-44400
ISBN 0-8161-7986-7

This publication is printed on permanent/durable acid-free paper
MANUFACTURED IN THE UNITED STATES OF AMERICA

Contents

Introduction vii

Acknowledgements xiii

Writings about Roger Williams, 1634-1974 1

Author Index 93

Selected Subject and Title Index 99

Introduction

Studies of the critical reputation of any literary figure present a number of questions in interpretation, influence, and understanding. They can be summed up with one question, however: why did the men or women of a certain period admire or despise a particular writer? The problem of finding an answer to this question is compounded when the writer is someone like Roger Williams, a man who became a controversial figure years before he emerged in print. In examining the vast amount of material written over the past three hundred years, one is amazed at the sheer bulk of studies that focus on the single event in Williams's life that would have made him historically famous even if he had not written or published anything. This event was the banishment of Roger Williams from Massachusetts Bay in 1635 for religious or political reasons or both, depending upon which writer one reads and whether he is attacking or defending the Bay Colony's actions. This attack upon and defense of Williams's banishment has preoccupied the great majority of critics and historians from Williams's day to the first third of this century.

I

Most of the early written reaction to Roger Williams in the seventeenth and eighteenth centuries are by the leaders of the Massachusetts Bay Colony or their descendents who sought to justify the ways of Puritan life especially with regard to the treatment of dissenting and troublesome influences in the early colony. Naturally, the relatively few references to him are almost all negative.

What is striking about the discussion of Roger Williams is that he merits so much attention from so many diverse sources considering his relatively short stay in the Bay Colony. Puritan historians, in general, used him as a prime example of the trials and tribulations that the theocratic state had to put up with in its infancy. Moreover, his name and story reappear in various journals, diaries, and letters indicating an unequalled degree of personal popularity in comparison with numerous other rebels and troublemakers.

Much of what can be legitimately called sources of "reputation" in this period are mainly short sketches and chapters rather than full length studies. No person or press in Massachusetts was to publish anything favorable about Roger Williams until well into the eighteenth century. The positive contributions he made were almost completely ignored by everyone for almost one hundred years after his banishment. If anyone in America knew anything about Roger Williams it was almost certainly his removal by the Puritan forefathers and his founding of Rhode Island and nothing else. For a man who had caused so much upheaval, his fame during these early years was limited to a small number of people in Rhode Island who championed him as the founder of religious liberty.

Only one writer before 1800, Isaac Backus, in A History of New England With Particular Reference to That Denomination of Christians Called Baptists (1777-96), shows any evidence of having read and understood some of Williams's writings. Backus' book and John Callender, in An Historical Discourse on the Civil and Religious Affairs of the Colony of Rhode Island (1738) are of greatest importance in the emergence of Williams as a figure worthy of serious consideration in the nineteenth century studies that were to follow. But at the end of the eighteenth century the decline of Puritanism, the American Revolution, and the Enlightenment brought a number of drastic changes in America's reaction to its heroes. Roger Williams was on the way to becoming a patriotic folk hero with whom a rather young country could readily identify their own concepts of individual liberties.

II

During the nineteenth century the critical reputation of Roger Williams changed in a number of ways from the earlier basically negative responses. The written reactions to Roger Williams can best be divided into three broad areas. First, there was a tendency to romanticize and even mythologize Williams into a pioneer fighter for democracy or an all-American religious hero. Second, there was a more rational approach that sought to appraise Williams more realistically and assess his contributions to the American way of life. Third, there were some rather weak negative attacks on Williams of the sort that had been made in the earlier period. Although there is always a danger in categorization and there is certainly a degree of overlap in these areas, they do serve to indicate the almost complete reversal of Williams's reputation in the nineteenth century and to suggest some of the wide variance in viewpoint among numerous writers in the period. An analysis of these areas will aid in understanding both the romantic and realistic reactions to Williams.

The very nature of the biographical details about Roger Williams's life and his struggles against the Puritan establishment would be enough to suggest why he became a hero in the eyes of many Americans almost overnight following the American Revolution. Banished from Boston and sent out into the wilderness of Rhode Island, Williams typified in many ways the struggle of the young democracy in a world as old as Europe and 'old England.' Many American historians, like

INTRODUCTION

George Bancroft in his History of the United States of America (1834), religious leaders, and even statesmen saw in Roger Williams's story a parallel to the fight for freedom in the American colonies and their own personal war for independence and the rights to freedom of speech, assembly, religion, and thought. Many of those who wrote about Williams were in search of an early American archetypal hero to illustrate and support the basic freedom-loving approach found in the writings of Jefferson, Adams, and Washington. For these writers, Roger Williams represented in many ways the original American hero, complete with suffering and personal experience in the defining of the relationship between the individual and the state. Here was an available historical personage from whom they could trace the development of the American democratic tradition.

Linking Roger Williams to the rise of democracy in America became the major preoccupation of many writers who sought the dual objective of erasing the blots on his reputation and elevating him to a pedestal of honor and renown. The pedestal was both literal and figurative; literal in the presentation to the Congress of the United States in January of 1872 of a statue of Roger Williams that remains on display in the United States Capitol; figurative in the many books and articles that created a legendary hero only vaguely resembling the historical figure of Roger Williams. Consequently, all of the hero-worshipping writers (like Bancroft, Stone, Tuckerman, Straus, and Benedict) are thesis-oriented: they attempt to prove a preconceived idea about Williams by seeing what they want to see in his life and deeds. The results of this thesis-orientation are numerous critical works that focus on Williams's life especially his banishment from Massachusetts Bay, and his contribution to the development of religious and personal freedom in America.

A brief, but important, negative response to Roger Williams appeared in the writings of several late-nineteenth-century critics who sought to deny the importance of Williams's views on religious toleration and to place the entire blame for his banishment on his political beliefs. The main spokesmen for this critical approach were Charles Deane, President of the Massachusetts Historical Society, John G. Palfrey, an historian, and Henry Martyn Dexter, a minister and editor of The Congregationalist. These writers asserted the justice of the magistrates of the Massachusetts Bay in defending the colony against Williams's attack on its political authority. The most detailed exposition of the subject was Henry Dexter's book, As to Roger Williams (1876).

Palfrey, Deane, and Dexter were all reacting to the attempt to romanticize Williams into something of a super religious hero. The facts and information brought into consideration by the de-romanticizers are valuable additions to an understanding of Williams, and they opened up numerous considerations about the milieu and mind of Roger Williams. These writers saw Williams as a Separatist and sought to distinguish his ideas from those of the Congregationalists. In addition they evoked a great deal of counter reaction that forced those who would deal with Williams into the realm of fact rather than the fanciful imaginings that characterized much of the earlier work on Williams.

A number of writers presented a more realistic appraisal of Williams. Their work includes biography, history, critical editions of the texts, and general as well as specialized studies of Roger Williams as a writer. The central contribution they made was their recognition of Roger Williams as both an historical and a literary figure. The critical response to Williams in the nineteenth century ends on the premise that twentieth century writers moved from: Roger Williams could not be dealt with as a representative of a later age because he was of the seventeenth century and was too perplexing to categorize simply.

III

The twentieth-century reaction to Roger Williams has been characterized in many areas by the same kinds of scholarly investigations that have typified the study of other Puritans. With the publication of Kenneth Murdock's Increase Mather (1925), Samuel Eliot Morison's Builders of the Bay Colony (1930), William Haller's The Rise of Puritanism (1938), and Perry Miller's The New England Mind: The Seventeenth Century (1939), many new avenues of investigation were opened up for a hitherto widely neglected and misunderstood period in American cultural and intellectual history. The writings on Roger Williams in the twentieth century demonstrate the distinct influence of this renaissance in colonial studies with the publication of biographies and literary, theological, political, historical, and even sociological studies. Recent Roger Williams studies have been philosophical and theological analyses of his thinking as a seventeenth century Puritan.

Obviously, many twentieth-century writers on Williams have provided a corrective gloss to the mythologizing of the previous era. They have established new facts about Williams's life and presented new insights into his personal and public roles. First appearing as doctoral and master's theses at American and foreign universities, many of these studies have been specialized in scope and have presented Roger Williams as a writer, theologian, and political leader. In addition, journal articles and brief notes have enhanced our awareness of the textual and interpretational problems of the writings.

As Perry Miller and others have observed, no one century is likely to have the last word on Roger Williams. At this point in the twentieth century, however, writers are beginning in many respects to understand Williams for the first time. The theological investigations of Calamandrei, Hunsaker, and Morgan are valuable not only to enlighten the modern reader about Williams but also indicate fruitful avenues of further investigation. In the realm of literature, Teunissen and Hinz's edition of A Key has opened up a new area of

Introduction

study. The investigations of Williams's typological thought, by Bercovitch, and Rosenmeier, suggest the need to read and understand Roger Williams on his own terms.

Understanding Williams and understanding the Puritans provide an awareness of his period and its people. This brief survey of the critical reception of Roger Williams offers both outlines of what has been written and guidelines for future studies of a man that has been shown to be more sinned against than sinning.

IV

Since the public protest of Roger Williams and his controversial banishment in 1636, Williams has become the focal point of another controversy in the numerous critical and historical writings about him and his stand against the magistrates of the Massachusetts Bay Colony. This bibliographical reference guide is an attempt to assemble all of the written assessments about Roger Williams and to present a brief summary of the contents of each. The volume is divided into three parts: Introduction, Annotated Bibliography, and Index. Because more has been written about Roger Williams than almost any other major Colonial American figure and because of the wide divergence of critical response to him, I have presented in the Introduction a brief survey of the direction of this critical reaction over the past three and a half centuries. This serves a twofold purpose: (1) it provides an introduction to the bibliography itself, and (2) it offers a barometer by which the scholar and general reader can view the various fluctuations in Williams's critical popularity through the centuries. What should appear obvious at once is the very controversial nature of the criticism about Williams and his place in American history and literature.

The bibliography is arranged chronologically by date of publication and includes all books and shorter writings about Roger Williams. Where no publication date is available, such as in the early sections on seventeenth and eighteenth century writings about Williams, I have used the generally accepted date of composition of the work in question. This is particularly true in some of the earliest works that offer a valuable contemporary insight on Williams but were never intended for publication. The annotation with each entry is intended to offer a concise summary of the major points of each book or shorter writing. My purpose here has been to supply information; no attempt has been made to provide a qualitative judgment about any of the entries. Each of the entries is arranged alphabetically within a given year ("A" books, "B" shorter writings) and is numbered. These numbers (1846.B1) are used in the Index for easy reference to a given entry.

Since this is the first bibliography of writings about Roger Williams, I have tried to be as inclusive as possible. No bibliography is ever complete and this one is no exception. I have included all works on Williams through 1974, but doubtless some have escaped notice and certainly additions will be made to the ever increasing areas of interest for Williams scholars. Just a cursory glance at the entries of the last thirty years will reveal the extent and depth of modern scholarship on Williams that may be nothing more than a preview of what is to come. I have seen all of the entries in one form or another except where noted. Any additions to this bibliography will be gratefully welcomed.

The "Selected Subject and Title Index" has been arranged alphabetically by the major divisions of subjects in Williams scholarship. Here, I have tried to list every item that pertains to the major subject heading as it is treated in either a book or shorter writing. For example, I have included under the title of "Biography" all of the major book length biographies of Williams but also the shorter chapter or article-length entries that pertain to his life or portions of it. Often these will direct the reader to a work that, while concerned with the historical place of Williams in America, provides valuable information about his life not otherwise available. The Index entry under "Biography" will also demonstrate the great number of critical appraisals written before the twentieth century that are solely concerned with Williams's life. Beyond this, I have indicated the names of key figures in Williams's life (e.g. John Cotton, John Winthrop, etc.) that have been the subject in part or in whole of critical writings about Williams. I have tried to make the "Selected Subject and Title Index" a useful scholarly tool and logical extension of the "Annotated Bibliography." In listing the authors I have included the original editors of The Complete Writings of Roger Williams's (1963) as separate entries for the valuable critical essays that preceed the various works of Williams they have also edited. In the "Annotated Bibliography" I have indicated the content of their essays for easy reference. Finally, I have exercised selection in indicating entries that deal with an analysis of Williams's writings. Where the entries provide a brief survey or in depth study of the writings they have been so noted under the title of that writing. Where the entries merely list Williams's writings with no comment, I have omitted them from the major entry. This seems the best way of bringing attention to the writings of Williams where attention has been paid to them by both critics and historians through the years.

Acknowledgments

Grateful acknowledgment is made to the many people at several libraries and institutions who assisted me in the compilation of this bibliographical reference guide. They are: the Boston Atheneum, the Boston Public Library, the Rhode Island Historical Society Library, the Massachusetts Historical Society Library, the John Carter Brown Library, the Rockefeller Library of Brown University, the Houghton and Widener Libraries of Harvard University, the Yale Divinity School Library, the University of Illinois Library, the Library of Teachers College, Columbia University, the University of Massachusetts Library at Amherst, the Robert Frost Library at Amherst College, the Smith College Library, the Mount Holyoke College Library, the Forbes Library, the American Antiquarian Society Library, the Mugar Library of Boston University, the Pennsylvania State University Library, the Northeastern University Library, the Southwest Baptist Theological Seminary Library, and finally the Library of the Dallas Theological Seminary.

Special thanks to Everett and Katherine Emerson, Mason Lowance, Robert Denn, John Teunissen, Evelyn Hinz, Joanna Walsh, Bradford Swan, Ute Bargmann, M. X. Lesser, Lloyd Skiffington, Paul Wermuth, Ray Blois, Milton Cantor, Charlotte Spivack, Deirdre Sockbeson, Nancy Chudacoff, Thomas J. Coyle, and most of all to Mary Coyle, who also typed the manuscript.

Writings about Roger Williams, 1634-1974

<u>1634 A BOOKS - NONE</u>

<u>1634 B SHORTER WRITINGS</u>

1   WOOD, WILLIAM. <u>New England's Prospects</u>. London. Reprinted, edited by H. W. Boynton. Boston, 1898, p. 97.
    Refers to Williams's work among the Indians in New England. Hopes "that he may be an instrument of good amongst them."

<u>1643 A BOOKS</u>

1   COTTON, JOHN. <u>A Letter of Mr. John Cottons Teacher of the Church in Boston, in New-England, to Mr. Williams a Preacher there</u>. London. Reprinted, <u>The Complete Writings of Roger Williams</u>, Vol. I. New York: Russell & Russell, 1963, pp. 295-311.
    Discusses Williams's banishment and the reasons for it. Cotton says, "civill banishment; for what was done by the Magistrates, in that kinde, was neither done by my counsell nor content, although I dare not deny the sentence passed to be righteous in the eyes of God." Distinguishes the fact that Williams's banishment was the result of his sinning against his own conscience and not a question of religious persecution. Cites evidence against Williams and the causes of his banishment from the Massachusetts Bay Colony.

<u>1643 B SHORTER WRITINGS - NONE</u>

<u>1647 A BOOKS</u>

1   COTTON, JOHN. <u>The Bloudy Tenent Washed and Made White in the Bloud of the Lambe</u>. London. Printed by Matthew Symmons.
    Explains that Williams was banished not only for his opinions but because of his "violent and tumultuous

1647

    (COTTON, JOHN)
        carriage against the Patent" of the colony. Distinguishes between persecuting against conscience and persecuting one, like Williams that sinned against his own conscience.

1647 B SHORTER WRITINGS

1   BRADFORD, WILLIAM. History of Plymouth Plantation, 1620-1647. Edited by Worthington C. Ford. 2 vols. Boston: Massachusetts Historical Society, 1912 and Little, Brown, 1856, pp. 310, 364, 432. See Index Vol. II.
        Describes Williams's stay at Plymouth and his work as teacher. Presents information about his treatment with Indians and role as peacemaker with them for the colonists. Discusses how Williams fell into "strange opinions, and from opinion to practice, which caused some controversy between church and him." Tells of his removal to Salem. See 1952.B3.

2   WARD, NATHANIEL. The Simple Cobler of Aggawam in America. London. Reprinted, edited by Paul M. Zall. Lincoln: University of Nebraska Press, 1969, p. 14.
        Refutes Williams's concept of religious liberty although Williams is not mentioned by name, "I can rather stand amazed then reply to this; it is an astonishment that the brains of men should be parboyl'd in such impious ignorance."

1649 A BOOKS - NONE

1649 B SHORTER WRITINGS

1   SAVAGE, JAMES, ed. Winthrop's Journal, History of New England, 1630-1649. 2 vols. Boston: Little, Brown and Company, 1853. I: 49-50, 69, 145, 174, 189-194, 265, 340, 345. II: 236-237.
        The best edition of Winthrop's Journal containing notes and an index to all of the references to Williams in the writings of Winthrop. Valuable explanatory notes. Records and comments on Williams's relationship with the Plymouth and Salem Churches, his Separatist views on religion, his questioning of the right of the magistrates to punish church offenders, his helpful work with the Indians, his advice and warnings to the Colony about Indian raids, as well as an important document Williams wrote about the Indian's right to the land settled by the English. Presents contemporary opinions about Williams and comments on his appearances before court and charges brought against him. Also includes notices of Williams's activities after his removal to Providence.

2   WINTHROP, JOHN. *Winthrop Papers, Volumes I-V*. Edited by Allyn B. Forbes. Boston: Massachusetts Historical Society, 1929-to date. III: 315; IV: 1, 25; VI: 86.

    Includes many of the letters written by Williams to Winthrop after his removal to Providence. Contains question by Winthrop as to what Williams had gained by his departure to Providence and Williams's reply. Also includes numerous letters written by Williams to Winthrop about the activities of the Indians and the policies of the Bay Colony. News of friends and enemies as well as questions of religious nature are included.

1653 A BOOKS - NONE

1653 B SHORTER WRITINGS

1   JOHNSON, EDWARD. *The Wonder-Working Providence of Scion's Savior in New England*. London. Reprinted, edited by J. Franklin Jameson. New York: Charles Scribner's Sons, 1910, pp. 122-123.

    Does not refer to Williams by name but to those who would "lock up the Sword of Civill Government for ever, especially in matters that concerne the foure first Commands of God."

1669 A BOOKS - NONE

1669 B SHORTER WRITINGS

1   MORTON, NATHANIEL. *New England's Memoriall*. Cambridge. 6th edition. Boston: Congregational Board of Publications, 1855, pp. 102-106.

    Describes Williams as a troublemaker who not "only persisted but grew more violent in his way." Also lists a detailed account of the various charges against Williams and points out that he was a "disturber of both the church and commonwealth."

1678 A BOOKS

1   FOX, GEORGE and JOHN BURNYEAT. *A New England Firebrand Quenched*.... London: n.p.

    Fox's answer to Williams's *George Fox Digg'd out of His Burrowes* containing refutations on Williams's arguments against the Quakers.

1678

1678 B SHORTER WRITINGS - NONE

1680 A BOOKS - NONE

1680 B SHORTER WRITINGS

1   HUBBARD, WILLIAM. <u>General History of New England</u>. Published, <u>Massachusetts Historical Society Collections</u>, 2nd ser. V, VI (1815). Reprinted, Boston: Charles C. Little and James Brown, 1848, pp. 202-213.
    Devoted to the story of Williams as a heretic. "Thus much was thought meet to insert here concerning the great and lamentable apostasy of Mr. Williams, that it may be a warning to all others to take heed of a gradual declining from God in them, lest they be left to run such a course as he hath done." Praises Williams's attack on Quakers as showing that "his root had not gone up as rotteness, nor his blossom as dust."

1702 A BOOKS - NONE

1702 B SHORTER WRITINGS

1   MATHER, COTTON. <u>Magnalia Christi Americana</u>. London. Reprinted with introduction and notes by Thomas Robbins, 2 vols. Hartford: Silus Andrus and Sons, 1852, II: 495-507.
    Considers Williams at length in <u>Book VII</u>, "Little Foxes; or the Spirit of Rigid Separatism in One Remarkable Zealot." Explores Williams's life in America and offers praise for his work with the Indians and the securing of the Rhode Island Charter. Cites Williams as "one of the first that made themselves notable by their opposition to the church-order of these plantations." Includes incident about removal of red cross from flag in Salem.

1739 A BOOKS - NONE

1739 B SHORTER WRITINGS

1   CALLENDER, JOHN. <u>An Historical Discourse on the Civil and Religious Affairs of the Colony of Rhode Island</u>. Boston: S. Kneeland and T. Green. Reprinted, Freeport: Books for Libraries Press, 1971, pp. 72-151; also, Romeo Elton, ed. <u>Rhode Island Historical Society Collections</u>, 4 (1838), 45-176.

Raises questions about the early accounts of Williams by the New England historians. Maintains that Williams "by the whole course and tenor of his life and conduct here, [appears] to have been one of the most disinterested men that ever lived, a most pious and heavenly minded soul." Emphasizes Williams's concept of religious liberty.

1747 A BOOKS - NONE

1747 B SHORTER WRITINGS

1   DOUGLASS, WILLIAM. A Summary Historical and Political of the British Settlement in America. 2 vols. Boston: Rogers and Fowle. II: 76-77.
    Brief notice of Williams's life and events connected with his banishment to Rhode Island.

2   NEAL, DANIEL. The History of New England. 2 vols. London: A. Ward. Second Edition. II: 233-34.
    Relies wholly on Mather for attitude and material on Williams. Offers opinion on Rhode Island as a place "first inhabited by the Sectaries who were banished from Boston and has been an Asylum of such persons since...."

1757 A BOOKS - NONE

1757 B SHORTER WRITINGS

1   BURKE, WILLIAM. An Account of the European Settlements in America. London. 2 vols. Reprinted, New York: Research Reprints, 1970.
    Presents brief biography of Williams and his role as founder and settler of Providence, Rhode Island.

1764 A BOOKS - NONE

1764 B SHORTER WRITINGS

1   HUTCHINSON, THOMAS. The History of the Colony and Province of Massachusetts Bay. Boston. Reprinted, edited by Lawrence S. Mayo. 2 vols. Cambridge: Harvard University Press, 1936. I: 35-36.
    Derives information about Williams from Mather, Bradford, and Winthrop. Observes, "After all that has been said of

Roger Williams: A Reference Guide

1764

 (HUTCHINSON, THOMAS)
  the actions of this person [Williams] while he was in Massachusetts, it ought for ever to be remembered in his honor, that, for forty years after, instead of showing any revengeful resentment against the colony from which he had been banished, he seems to have been continually employed in acts of kindness and benevolence...."

1771 A BOOKS - NONE

1771 B SHORTER WRITINGS

1 HOPKINS, STEPHEN. An Historical Account of the Planting and Growth of Providence. Edited by William E. Foster. Rhode Island Historical Society Collections, VII (1885), 47-52.
 Unfinished history of Rhode Island in which the treatment of Williams is contrasted with the earlier writings of New England historians who "represented the inhabitants of this colony as a company of people who lived without order...and this principally because they allowed an unlimited liberty of conscience." Discusses role of Williams as leader of early colony.

1777 A BOOKS - NONE

1777 B SHORTER WRITINGS

1 BACKUS, ISAAC. A History of New England With Particular Reference To That Denomination of Christians Called Baptists. 2 vols. Newton, Mass.: Backus Historical Society, 1877. Reprinted, New York: Arno Press, 1969. I: vii-viii, 255-257, 414.
 Systematic examination of Williams's life and writings focusing on a refutation of act of banishment at hands of Bay magistrates. Concludes about Williams that "His great crime therefore was his advancing such questions as he did, against the power, which, in plain terms, was a power to frame themselves a gospel and a Christ without a cross; a power to suspend obedience to what they looked upon to be truth in England...."

2 ROBERTSON, WILLIAM. The History of America. London. Philadelphia, 1822, p. 254.
 Distinguishes the differences between Williams and other Puritans of the period. "His spirit differed from that of the Puritans in Massachusetts; it was mild and tolerating;

and having ventured himself to reject established opinions, he endeavoured to secure the same liberty to other men...." A brief discussion of other people and events connected with Providence settlement.

1778 A BOOKS - NONE

1778 B SHORTER WRITINGS

1   RUSSELL, WILLIAM. The History Of America. Philadelphia: James Humphreys, pp. 159, 176.
    Includes brief biography and history of Williams's role in settlement of Providence.

1780 A BOOKS - NONE

1780 B SHORTER WRITINGS

1   CHALMERS, GEORGE. Political Annals of the Present United Colonies. London, pp. 156, 269 ff.
    Maintains that Williams was a preacher of the "wildest doctrine in religion and government...always fruitful in religious frenzies." Role of Williams was detrimental to peace and harmony in early years of Massachusetts Bay Colony.

1794 A BOOKS - NONE

1794 B SHORTER WRITINGS

1   MASSACHUSETTS HISTORICAL SOCIETY. "A Key Into the Language of America," Massachusetts Historical Society Collections, III: 203-238, V: 80-106.
    First reprinting of Williams's treatise on the Indians presented only excerpts from the original and those representing it as a linguistic and cultural record without any of the criticism of English. Became only edition of Williams's work in print for next thirty years.

1810 A BOOKS - NONE

1810 B SHORTER WRITINGS

1   TRUMBULL, BENJAMIN. A General History of the United States of

1810

    (TRUMBULL, BENJAMIN)
       America. 3 vols. Boston: Farrand, Mallory and Co. I: 105.
        Brief treatment of Williams. Praises his actions and finds his contribution to America important.

1813 A BOOKS - NONE

1813 B SHORTER WRITINGS

1   BENEDICT, DAVID. General History of the Baptist Denomination in America. 2 vols. Boston: Lincoln & Edmunds. I: 354-355, II: 273-277.
     Presents evidence to prove Williams was a Baptist and that the "fear of the consequences of his popular ministry induced the priest-led magistrates to pass the cruel sentence of banishment against him." Argues that Williams remained a Baptist for several years and not just several months as has been believed.

1818 A BOOKS - NONE

1818 B SHORTER WRITINGS

1   RAMSAY, DAVID. History of the United States. 2 vols. 2nd edition. Philadelphia. I: 183.
     Discusses Williams's "blind zeal" and praises his ideals that were "afterwards admired in the writings of Milton, Locke, and Furneau."

1819 A BOOKS - NONE

1819 B SHORTER WRITINGS

1   EVANS, JOHN. Memoirs of the Life and Writings of the Rev. William Richardson...with some account of the Rev. Roger Williams, founder of the state of Rhode Island as well as the first assertor of complete Religious Liberty in the United States of America. Chiswick: C. Whittingham, pp. 323-396.
     One of the earliest lives of Williams. Contains brief story of dates and facts connected with his life and focuses mainly on his contributions to religious liberty. Contains some errors and inaccuracies in dates and places.

1827 A BOOKS - NONE

1827 B SHORTER WRITINGS

1   RHODE ISLAND HISTORICAL SOCIETY. "Introduction" to "A Key Into The Language of America," Rhode Island Historical Society Publications. I: 9-16.
    Offers very brief introduction to Williams's work and biographical background of it. "In regard to the literary attainments of Roger Williams it is deemed to say but little. The readers of this work will be principally such as chuse to form their own opinions. It will be, however, generally admitted, that his Style abounds with the Beauties and Defects, peculiar to the Literature of his own Times. It is no small praise to say of him, that, as an author, he compares well with his great opponent, Cotton." Text of A Key follows this introduction to Williams's work, pp. 17-163.

1832 A BOOKS

1   DURFEE, JOB. Whatcheer, or Roger Williams in Banishment. A Poem. Providence: Cranston & Hammond.
    An epic poem written in nine cantos of about fifty stanzas each. Depicts Williams's deeds as a wilderness hero among the Indians. Title from the expression Williams greeted the Indians with on his arrival in Providence. Williams portrayed as epic hero.

1832 B SHORTER WRITINGS - NONE

1833 A BOOKS - NONE

1833 B SHORTER WRITINGS

1   ANON. "Annotations of a Bibliographer, Williams' Key-Allen's Narrative," North American Magazine, 2, No. 9 (July).
    Brief article dealing with the publication of Williams's Key Into The Language of America by the Rhode Island Historical Society in 1827. Includes the "Poetry" and "Observations" sections of A Key and also importance of the work as a study of early Indian languages and customs.

1834 A BOOKS
    1   KNOWLES, JAMES D. Memoir of Roger Williams. Boston: Lincoln & Edmunds.

1834

(KNOWLES, JAMES D.)
First full-length biography of Williams. Examines letters and other writings of Williams in analyzing his life. Contains earliest study of correspondence between Williams and Winthrop. Uses much contemporary evidence in discussion of Williams. Concludes, "Mr. Williams was unnecessarily scrupulous about some minor points of conduct and of policy, though these scruples may be candidly traced to the agregated conditions of the public mind in England and America, and to his own delicacy of conscience." Extensive survey of earlier writings about Williams contained in Preface.

1834 B SHORTER WRITINGS

1   PARKMAN, F. "Review of Memoir of Roger Williams," Christian Examiner, 16 (March), 72-97.
    Essay review of Knowles' biography of Williams comments on style, objectivity, and contents of book. Discusses issue of banishment and presents a survey of early nineteenth-century reactions to Williams. Includes text of letter of Williams on the subject of toleration.

1838 A BOOKS - NONE

1838 B SHORTER WRITINGS

1   FOSTER, JOHN. "Roger Williams in Banishment," Eclectic Review, 68 (January), 22-41.
    Review of Job Durfee's poem Whatcheer, or Roger Williams in Banishment (See 1832.A1).

2   HINMAN, ROYAL RALPH. The Blue Laws of New Haven Colony....
    Hartford: Case, Tiffany, & Company, pp. 63-67.
    In a section on the trial of Williams, Hinman quotes the charges against Williams from Winthrop's Journal. Shows how banishment of Williams is in many ways similar to the treatment of Joseph in the Bible. Finally, asserts important work Williams did in the settlement of Providence and in the founding of the first Baptist church in America in Rhode Island. Finds it hard to even imagine that Williams was so harshly treated by fellow Christians and looks upon incident as a sad indication of Puritan intolerance at its worst.

1839 A BOOKS

1   JOHNSON, LORENZO. The Spirit of Roger Williams. Boston: Cassady and March.
    Presents biography of Williams and his efforts in developing concept of soul liberty. Asserts, "we have not yet imbibed his philosophy in its full extent, and, hence, it is, that the name which future ages shall revere as that of the noblest apostle in the cause of soul's freedom in modern ages is but imperfectly known." Briefly summarizes other writings about Williams including Knowles.

1839 B SHORTER WRITINGS

1   Z. Z. Z. "Roger Williams," Yale Literary Magazine, 4 (Feb.), 153-160.
    Laments the poor reputation of Williams after his death. Examines the details of Williams's early life and his banishment. Analyzes his writings and comments on the style. Cites Williams's contributions in the areas of theology, letters, and politics as significant. Closes with discussion of his important principle of freedom of religion.

1840 A BOOKS - NONE

1840 B SHORTER WRITINGS

1   ANON. "Cofiant Roger Williams," Y Cyfaill, XXVII (March), iii, 65-67.
    Brief article written in Welsh dealing with Williams's origins in Wales and evidence about birth, etc. Copy in Brown University Library.

1843 A BOOKS - NONE

1843 B SHORTER WRITINGS

1   BANCROFT, GEORGE. History of the United States. 2 vols. Boston. Tenth Edition. I: 254-55, 366, 375-77.
    Relates Williams to the rise of democracy in America by showing his influence as one of the earliest liberal democrats. Credits Williams as "the first person in modern Christendom to establish civil government on the doctrine of liberty of conscience, the equality of opinions before the law; and in its defence he was the harbinger of Milton, the precursor and superior of Jeremy Taylor." Sees Williams

1843

    (BANCROFT, GEORGE)
        as one who advanced the cause of both moral and political science and "made himself a benefactor of his race."

2   WHIPPLE, FRANCIS H. "Landing of Roger Williams," <u>The New Mirror</u>, II, no. 17 (Jan. 27), 1.
        Picture of Williams landing in Providence in 1636 accompanied by twenty-four line poem by Whipple celebrating deeds of "Illustrious pioneer of liberty" and comparing Williams with William Penn. Drawing is by Hoppin.

<u>1845 A BOOKS</u>

1   GAMMELL, WILLIAM. <u>Life of Roger Williams, Founder of the State of Rhode Island</u>. Boston: Kendall & Lincoln.
        Contains information taken from Knowles' biography (1834.A1) as well as a brief treatment of incidents. "In selecting and arranging the materials, which are thus supplied, the aim of the present writer has been to confine himself to those which are best fitted to illustrate the personal character of this eminent man, and to furnish the means of estimating aright the services he rendered to his own and subsequent times." Contains appendix with summation of Williams's writings "presented to the attention of readers who may be curious about such things."

<u>1845 B SHORTER WRITINGS</u>

1   MACKIE, J. M. "Roger Williams," <u>North American Review</u>, 61 (January), 1-20.
        Review of Gammell's biography (1845.A1) with large sections of quotes from it. Adds further praise of Williams's deeds. Sees Williams as far in advance of his time.

<u>1846 A BOOKS</u>

1   UNDERHILL, EDWARD BEAN, ed. <u>The Bloudy Tenent of Persecution</u>. London: Hanserd Knollys Society.
        Edition of Williams's work contains thirty page introduction and index to text. Primarily concerned with biography of Williams, and his relationship to the concept of religious freedom.

<u>1846 B SHORTER WRITINGS - NONE</u>

1847 A BOOKS - NONE

1847 B SHORTER WRITINGS

1   GROSVENOR, CYRUS PITT. Review of Correspondence of Messrs. Fuller and Wayland...to which is added a discourse on "The Hireling Ministry". Utica: Christian Contributor's Office. Appendix.
      Brief introduction to Williams's Hireling Ministry citing his contributions to the idea of religious liberty. "Few men of any age have left in the world's mind a more permanent impression."

1850 A BOOKS

1   ADLAM, SAMUEL. The First Church in Providence, Not the Oldest of the Baptists in America. Newport: Cranston and Norman's Power Press.
      Contends that the Newport, Rhode Island, Baptist Church was the first in America and that Williams was not founder of the Newport Church and maybe not even the Providence church. Presents evidence about Williams to support assertions.

1850 B SHORTER WRITINGS - NONE

1851 A BOOKS - NONE

1851 B SHORTER WRITINGS

1   UNDERHILL, EDWARD BEAN. Struggles and Triumphs of Religious Liberty: An Historical Survey of Controversies Pertaining to the Rights of Conscience from the English Reformation to the Settlement of New England. New York: Lewis Colby, pp. 216-240.
      Section XI contains a study of Williams and a biography of him. Examines Williams's controversy with Cotton and sees his persecution by the Puritans as a direct result of his religious beliefs. Analysis of Bloudy Tenent.

1852 A BOOKS - NONE

1852 B SHORTER WRITINGS

1   ALLEN, REV. R. W. "Roger Williams," Methodist Quarterly Review, 12 (April), 199-212.

1852

(ALLEN, REV. R. W.)
Review of Knowles (1834.A1) and Gammell (1845.A1) biographies of Williams. Includes brief biography of Williams and listing of his writings and locations of copies of them. Concludes that because Williams was so important a new edition is needed of his writings.

1853 A BOOKS

1   ELTON, ROMEO. Life of Roger Williams. Providence: G. H. Whitney.
    Biography of Williams designed for exclusively English audience. Depends heavily on Knowles' biography (1834.A1) and acknowledges this in preface. Tends to be less annotated and offers fewer letters by and about Williams.

1853 B SHORTER WRITINGS

1   GERVINUS, GEORG GOTTFRIED. "Introduction," in A History of the Nineteenth Century Year by Year. London: H. G. Bohn, p. 65.
    Brief statement of the importance of Williams and the successful experiment in Providence as an example of democracy with religious freedom. Singles out the importance of Williams's contribution to both America and the world.

1855 A BOOKS – NONE

1855 B SHORTER WRITINGS

1   BARRY, JOHN S. The History of Massachusetts. 3 vols. Boston: Phillips, Samson, and Company. I: 235-244.
    Treats Williams's banishment in some detail. Judges actions of magistrates were unjustifiable and describes Williams as "probably as bright a character as any in New England."

2   FELT, JOSEPH. The Ecclesiastical History of New England. 2 vols. Boston: Congregational Board of Publication. I: 232-238.
    Presents sympathetic discussion of Williams. He finds that Williams's presence was very troublesome to the early magistrates.

1857 A BOOKS – NONE

1857 B SHORTER WRITINGS

1   BELL, J. D. "The Sanctity of Conscience, Roger Williams," <u>Ladies Repository</u>, 17 (May), 289-292.
    Cites key idea in Williams's thought as his concept of religious liberty as a reflection of his sanctity of the conscience. This was the focus of his dispute with the Massachusetts Bay.

2   ELLIOTT, CHARLES W. <u>The New England History, from the Discovery of the Continent</u>.... 2 vols. New York: Charles Scribner's. I: 201-205.
    Sees Williams as a sacrificial victim of the persecutions by the Bay magistrates. Brief discussion of life of Williams prior to his banishment.

3   TUCKERMAN, HENRY T. "Roger Williams: The Tolerant Colonist," in <u>Essays Biographical and Critical, or Studies in Character</u>. Boston: Phillips Samson & Company, pp. 181-190.
    Discusses Williams as "one of those rare combinations of saint and hero." Analyzes Williams's writings by saying, "Of his mental powers we have no means of judging, except the respect and interest he awakened in those with whom he dwelt, and the writings he left. These are chiefly of a controversial nature, and on questions which have, in great measure, lost their significance. The style, too, is involved, quaint and often pedantic. The views, however, advocated even in his polemic discussions are often in advance of his time, and the sentiments he professes are noble and progressive...."

1858 A BOOKS - NONE

1858 B SHORTER WRITINGS

1   GRAVES, J. R. <u>Trials and Sufferings For Religious Liberty in New England</u>. Nashville: Graves Marks & Co.
    Cites Williams as one of the many famous examples of Puritan treatment of dissenters. Brief exposition of his life in the Massachusetts Bay and the trials he endured.

2   PALFREY, JOHN GORHAM. <u>A History of New England</u>. 3 vols. Boston: Houghton Mifflin. I: 412-418.
    Does not deny the "sound and generous principle of a perfect freedom of conscience in religious concerns" but argues that these had nothing to do with Williams's banishment from the Massachusetts Bay Colony. "As long as he

1858

    (PALFREY, JOHN GORHAM)
    [Williams] was in Massachusetts, he was no heretic, tried by the standards of the time and place. He was not charged with heresy. The questions which he raised, and by raising which he provoked opposition on, were questions relating to the political rights and to the administration of government."

*3 SEYMOUR, C. C. B. "Roger Williams," in <u>Self-made Men</u>. New York: Harper and Brothers, Inc., p. 275.
[Cited in C. S. Brigham, <u>Bibliography of Rhode Island History</u>, 1902. Not seen.]

1859 A BOOKS

1 ARNOLD, SAMUEL GREEN. <u>History of the State of Rhode Island and Providence Plantations</u>. 2 vols. New York: D. Appleton and Company. Vol. I.
Deals with Williams's role in founding and settling of the colony of Rhode Island. Offers documents and detailed analysis of Williams's role in securing the charter for the colony. Offers perspective on Williams in relation to other early settlers of the colony. Discussion of Williams in Vol. I, with early history of state.

1859 B SHORTER WRITINGS

1 MASSON, DAVID. <u>Life of Milton</u>. 6 vols. London. Vol. II: 555-63, 573; Vol. III: 116; Vol. IV: 395-96.
Earliest explanation of Williams's concept of Separatism and his relationship with the English poet John Milton. Specific discussions of Milton and Williams.

1860 A BOOKS

1 ALLEN, ZACHARIAH. <u>Memorial of Roger Williams</u>. Paper read before the Rhode Island Historical Society, May 18. Providence. n.p.
Discusses plans to erect a monument to Williams. Main emphasis on Williams's concept of soul liberty. The dispute with Bay magistrates was one of their failure to see Williams's humanitarian feelings toward the Indians. Urges need for monument to be erected to memory of such a great person.

2 McDOUGALL, FRANCES, ed. Roger Williams, An Extract From an Unpublished Poem by Fanny Green. New York.
  The poem entitled "Nananantinoo" depicts Williams's life among the Indians. Copy in Rhode Island Historical Society Library. Discusses role of Williams.

1860 B SHORTER WRITINGS

1 SHERMAN, DAVID. "Roger Williams," in Sketches of New England Divines. New York: Carlton & Porter, pp. 34-56.
  Fundamental importance of understanding Williams's character as the basis of his ideas of religious liberty. "While we do not claim for him [Williams] an exemption from human frailties, we do claim that those frailties not only hold an inferior place, but properly disappear on the page of history amid the splendor of his good qualities." Presents Williams as a character having a great deal of work to do in beating back harsh Puritans.

2 ROGER WILLIAMS MONUMENT ASSOCIATION. An Act To Incorporate the Roger Williams Monument Association of the State of Rhode Island and Providence Plantations. Providence. Copy in Rhode Island Historical Society Library.
  Legal framework of association formed for erection of monument to Williams.

3 WAYLAND, FRANCIS. "Dr. Wayland on Roger Williams." New York, The World (16 June), p. 1.
  Presents the speech of Dr. Wayland at the recent meeting of the Roger Williams's Monument Association. Praises Williams for his deeds and ranks him with Milton and Cromwell. Cites Williams's work as a religious leader as part of his contribution to America. Calls upon all Rhode Islanders to contribute to the work of erecting this monument to such an outstanding figure.

1861 A BOOKS

1 EDDY, D. C. Roger Williams and the Baptists: An Historical Discourse. Boston: Andrew F. Groves
  Outlines a capsule history of the Baptist movement and identifies several of its characteristics with Williams. Shows the distinguishing tenets of the faith and the important influence of these upon various governments, nations, and religions. Demonstrates how Williams's ideas of religious liberty were important in the development of religious freedom in America. Sees all of Williams's ideas on religious liberty as indebted to his Baptist faith.

Roger Williams: A Reference Guide

1861

1861 B SHORTER WRITINGS

1   ANON. "The Apple Tree Root Story," Providence Herald, Weekly Novelette (16 Feb.), p. 366.
      Deals with the discovery of an apple tree that had formed its roots around grave of Williams. When body was removed to monument, discovery was made of strange formation around Williams's skeleton.

1862 A BOOKS

1   RIDER, SIDNEY S., ed. Experiments of Spiritual Life and Health. Providence: S. S. Rider.
      Calls attention to similarities between Williams and Richard Baxter in this type of treatise. Discusses content of Williams's treatise. Explains how treatise was discovered.

2   GUILD, REUBEN ALDRIDGE. An Account of the Writings of Roger Williams. Providence: Brown University.
      Summarizes and details the chronology of Williams's writings. Relates specific events in Williams's life with the publication of his writings. Includes those writings published in The Writings of Roger Williams (1866.A1).

1862 B SHORTER WRITINGS

1   ASPINWALL, THOMAS. "The Narragansett Patent," Proceedings Massachusetts Historical Society, 6 (June), 41-77.
      Examines Deane (1873.B1) regarding the validity of the Narragensett Patent adopted by Massachusetts to forbid Williams to exercise "jurisdiction in Providence and the Island of Quiday." Explains Williams's position by letter of 27 August 1645.

1864 A BOOKS - NONE

1864 B SHORTER WRITINGS

1   ARNOLD, SAMUEL GREEN. "Roger Williams," in Illustrated Pilgrim Memorial. Plymouth, Massachusetts: The Pilgrim Society, p. 23.
      Briefly discusses role of Williams among the pilgrim fathers as related in Bradford's history (1647.B1). Shows how Williams lived in peace with Indians.

1866

2 BARTLETT, JOHN RUSSELL. Bibliography of Rhode Island. Providence: Alfred Anthony, pp. 272-282.
   Contains listing of writings by Williams as well as the location of some editions of his works. Includes brief description of each work.

1866 A BOOKS

1 BARTLETT, JOHN RUSSELL, ed. "Introduction," The Letters of Roger Williams. Vol. VI, The Writings of Roger Williams. Providence: Narragansett Club Publications, pp. ix-xi.
   Contains information on the assembly and location of letters by Williams. Also introduces some persons mentioned in them.

2 CALDWELL, SAMUEL L., ed. "Introduction," The Bloudy Tenent of Persecution. Vol. III, The Writings of Roger Williams. Providence: Narragansett Club Publications. III: pp. iii-xiv.
   Contains background information on treatise and response of John Cotton to it. Brief study of form and types of arguments in work.

3 CHILD, ANNE P. Whatcheer, A Story of Olden Times. Providence: Knowles Anthony & Company.
   Fictional story of Roger Williams among the Indians. Based in part on facts taken from Elton's Life of Williams (See 1853.A1).

4 DIMAN, REV. J. LEWIS, ed. "Introduction," George Fox Digg'd out of His Burrowes. Vol. V, The Writings of Roger Williams. Providence: Narragansett Club Publications. V, pp. iii-lviii.
   Presents information about Williams's debate with Fox and the content of the arguments advanced. Also biography of Williams at the time of the debate.

5 GUILD, REUBEN ALDRIDGE, ed. "Biographical Introduction," in Vol. I, The Writings of Roger Williams. Providence: Narragansett Club Publications. I: pp. 1-60.
   Biography of Williams based in large part on the recent works of Knowles, Gammell, and Elton. Cites the important contributions of Williams to the concept of religious liberty.

6 _____. "Introduction," Mr. Cotton's Letter Examined and Answered, Vol. I, The Writings of Roger Williams. Providence: Narragansett Club Publications. I: pp. 287-294.

Roger Williams: A Reference Guide

1866

    (GUILD, REUBEN ALDRIDGE)
       Background information on letter and Williams's answer to it. Brief chronology of Williams's life.

7   TRUMBULL, JAMES HAMMOND, ed. "Introduction," A Key Into the Language of America. Vol. I, The Writings of Roger Williams. Providence: Narragansett Club Publications. I: pp. 63-76.
      Examination of the linguistic materials in A Key and the events related to its composition. Discusses Williams's work with the Indians and printing history of A Key.

1866 B SHORTER WRITINGS

1   M'CARTY, REV. J. H. "Roger Williams," Ladies Repository, 26 (Sept.), 513-516; (Oct.), 593-597.
      Two-part essay contains a biography of Williams and an analysis of his writings. Points out the importance of Williams's ideas to the later development of religious liberty in America. Explains that Williams's ideas of religious liberty have not been well known or recognized for their importance.

2   UPHAM, W. P. "An Account of the Dwelling Place of Francis Higginson, Samuel Skelton, Roger Williams, and Hugh Peters," Essex Institute Historical Collections, 8, No. 4 (April).
      Discusses the details and history of the parsonage in Salem, Massachusetts, where Williams lived for a period during his ministry.

1867 A BOOKS - NONE

1867 B SHORTER WRITINGS

1   EDWARDS, MORGAN. "Materials for a History of the Baptists of Rhode Island," Rhode Island Historical Society Collections, 6: 306, 317-18.
      Though not complete, this work, written in the eighteenth century, marks one of the earliest attempts to tell Williams's story. Offers brief life of Williams and his founding of colony of Rhode Island.

2   PURNELL, T. R. "Roger Williams," in Literature and Its Professors. London: Bell and Daldy, pp. 164-191.
      Examines Williams's life in "The Man of Letters as A Statesman." One of the earliest written analyses of Williams's writings. Gives biography of Williams followed by an analysis of his writings with emphasis on The Bloudy

Tenent and The Hireling Ministry. "His writings are amongst the dreariest of the dreary productions that appeared during the commonwealth. Everything he wrote, if we except his philological work, "A Vocabulary of the Narragansett Language,"...is occupied with considerations of minute and unimportant points of controversy, which...have now altogether ceased to be of interest...."

1869 A BOOKS - NONE

1869 B SHORTER WRITINGS

*1   SCOTT, M. B. "Roger Williams not the author of the first recorded agreement in Rhode Island Securing liberty of conscience," Dawson Historical Magazine, 16: 226-28.
   [Cited in C. S. Brigham, Bibliography of Rhode Island History, 1902. Not seen.]

1870 A BOOKS - NONE

1870 B SHORTER WRITINGS

1   UPHAM, W. P. "The House of Roger Williams, 1635," Bulletin of the Essex Institute, 2 (April), 55-60.
   Discusses the house in Salem, Massachusetts where Williams was living just prior to his banishment from the Bay Colony. Points out that this was not the parsonage belonging to the Salem church but a private house that Williams sold to a friend in order to avoid confiscation of the house and property when he left for the Rhode Island colony.

1871 A BOOKS

1   MUDGE, REV. Z. A. Footprints of Roger Williams: A Biography with Sketches of Important Events in Early New England History with which he was Connected. New York: Carlton & Lanahan.
   A biography of Williams written for young children. Surveys early books on Williams and states: "But none of these are professedly written for young people, for whom especially this volume is prepared...We desire that our Footprints may inspire in the young a wish for a further acquaintance with the thrilling events and noble characters of early American history." Also focuses on events in early New England with which Williams was concerned.

1871

1871 B SHORTER WRITINGS

1 BRADLEY, C. S. "Roger Williams," speech at Plymouth Celebration, December 21, 1870. Providence: <u>Providence Journal</u> (January 7, 1871), p. 1.
   Speech given at 250th celebration of settlement at Plymouth, Massachusetts. Deals with Williams's role in early colony and work with Indians.

1872 A BOOKS

1 DENISON, REVEREND FREDERIC. <u>Soul Liberty: An Historical Poem</u>. Mystic, Conn., n.p.
   Presents Williams as a hero of religious liberty and the importance of his contribution to our world. Copy in Brown University Library, Providence.

2 STONE, THOMAS T. <u>Roger Williams, The Prophetic Legislator</u>. Providence: A. C. Greene.
   Reprint of speech delivered before Rhode Island Historical Society, November 8, 1871. Attempts to cover "not so much the story as the character, the service, the idea of Roger Williams." After analyzing historical character of Williams, goes on to say, "Let us endeavor now to translate it into its genuine significance, the living idea which in the growth of our nation and in the progress of humanity he [Williams] brought into manifestation and distinct action." Refers to Williams's "conscientious contentiousness" as an important factor in understanding his sense of soul freedom.

1872 B SHORTER WRITINGS

1 BRONSON, B. F. "Roger Williams and Palfrey," <u>The Baptist Quarterly</u>, 6 (April), 156-166.
   Refutes the arguments of Palfrey (<u>See</u> 1858.B2) that Williams was banished from the Massachusetts Bay Colony for strictly political reasons. Demonstrates that Palfrey has misrepresented the facts in relation to Williams and his idea of religious liberty.

2 CALDWELL, SAMUEL L. "Roger Williams As Author," <u>The Baptist Quarterly</u>, 6 (April), 385-407.
   A description of the various works of Williams as they were being assembled for <u>The Writings</u> (1966.A1-A2, A4-A7). Deals with a summary of the contents of each work and the location of the various texts. Selections from <u>A Key</u>.

1875

3   EAMES, B. T. "Statue of Roger Williams," speech in House of Representatives, Washington, D. C., January 11, in Henry B. Anthony, Memorial Addresses on Several Occasions. Providence: n.p., 1875.
    Delivered on the presentation of the statue of Roger Williams to the United States Congress. Voices words of gratitude for Williams's role in the development of religious liberty in America. Cites reasons for the need and justification of a statue to Williams in the capitol.

4   UNITED STATES CONGRESS. Proceedings in Congress, 1872. Washington, D. C.
    Program and ceremonies marking the official presentation and acceptance of the statue of Williams to the United States. Contains speeches and dedications of the various speakers from both Rhode Island and other states.

1873 A BOOKS - NONE

1873 B SHORTER WRITINGS

1   DEANE, CHARLES. "Roger Williams and the Massachusetts Charter," Proceedings Massachusetts Historical Society, 12: 341-358.
    Suggests that Williams's attack on the Massachusetts charter was misdirected. "It seems to me that Williams clearly misinterprets the language of the patent...the objection of Williams to the patent seems to have been merely theoretical questions." Further disputes Williams's charter in Rhode Island by observing that Williams probably found opposing government one thing and running a government quite another.

1874 A BOOKS

1   MILLER, CHARLES T. Settlement of Rhode Island. Providence: Graphic Company.
    Collection of cartoon illustrations by Walter F. Brown to accompany Miller's song about Williams and the discovery of Providence. Points out Williams's friendship with Indians and various events connected with early settlement.

1874 B SHORTER WRITINGS - NONE

1875 A BOOKS - NONE

1875

1875 B SHORTER WRITINGS

1 ANTHONY, HENRY B. "Remarks on Presentation of the Statue of of Roger Williams" in <u>Memorial Addresses on Several Occasions</u>. Providence: n. p.

   Contains address delivered January 9, 1872, by Senator Anthony at the dedication of the statue of Williams in Washington, D. C. Praised Williams as "not merely laying the foundations of religious freedom, he [Williams] constructed the whole edifice, in all its impregnable strength, in all its imperishable beauty." Describes Williams's role in the development of religious liberty and his contribution to freedom in America.

2 DEXTER, HENRY MARTYN. "Roger Williams," <u>Congregationalist</u>, 60 (6 May).

   Presents information to show the real reasons that Williams was banished from Massachusetts. Assembly of many accounts of Williams from the original sources of John Cotton, John Winthrop, William Bradford, and Edward Winslow to show why Williams was banished and show that the recent biographies of Backus (1777.B1), Knowles (1834.A1), Gammell (1845.A1), and Elton (1853.A1) do not present the facts from the original sources. Concludes that Williams's concept of soul liberty was not the reason for his banishment. Also includes information on the correct date of banishment for Williams as October 8, 1635.

3 DUYCKINCK, EVERT A. and GEORGE L. <u>Cyclopedia of American Literature</u>. 2 vols. Philadelphia: William Rutter. I: 37-43.

   Extended commentary on Williams's works, particularly <u>The Bloudy Tenent</u>. Praises Williams as a true "poet" in both his private and controversial works. Includes extensive selections from <u>Tenent</u> as well as the important correspondence between Williams and Mrs. Sadleir in summary form. Early examination of both the ideas in Williams's writings and the contexts of them. Also refers to body of letters written by Williams, and the personality revealed by them. Concludes with statement of Williams's contributions to American literature.

1876 A BOOKS

1 DEXTER, HENRY MARTYN. <u>As to Roger Williams and His 'Banishment' from the Massachusetts Plantation</u>. Boston: Congregational Publication Society.

An effort "to go straight to the original sources, and candidly, and in detail, to examine them, and make up a judgment upon them; without regard to the rhetoric of superficial biographers, or prejudiced historians, or the misapprehensions of a later public sentiment by them misled." Sees Williams's banishment as a result of political problem Williams posed for magistrates and not religious question at all. Extensive use of original source materials about Williams in both England and America. "It was his bitterly separative spirit which began and kept alive the difficulty, --not theirs. He withdrew communion from them--not they from him....In all strictness and honesty he [Williams] persecuted them - not they him." Concludes by refuting claim that Williams was first Baptist martyr in America.

1876 B SHORTER WRITINGS

1 BARROWS, C. E. "Roger Williams," The Baptist Quarterly, 10 (Oct.), 353-361.
Argues against position advocated by Dexter (1876.A1). Discusses the importance of understanding the separation of church and state as central to Williams's thought. Sees Dexter's conclusions as incorrect.

2 CLARKE, J. C. C. "Roger Williams and Rhode Island," The Baptist Quarterly, 10 (Oct.), 183-204, 257-281.
Argues that John Clarke and not Williams was the founder of the first Baptist church in America. The honors have gone unjustly to Williams in the past.

3 FOORD, JOHN. "Religious Liberty in the United States," New York Times, (14 May), p. 7.
A negative review of Dexter's book (1876.A1). Maintains that Williams's contributions to religious liberty have yet to be realized and that Dexter has done an injustice to historical scholarship. Advances case for Williams as an apostle of liberty and cites reasons for his importance.

1877 A BOOKS

1 DIMAN, J. LOUIS. Address at Unveiling of Monument to Roger Williams. Providence: H. Angell & Co.
Contains speech of Diman on Williams's contributions to Providence and religious liberty in general. Also contains the ceremonies and speeches by other dignataries on the unveiling of the monument to Williams in Providence, Rhode Island. Diman's speech was the main oration for the occasion.

Roger Williams: A Reference Guide

1877

1877 B SHORTER WRITINGS

1 GREENE, GEORGE WASHINGTON. <u>A Short History of Rhode Island</u>. Providence: J. A. & R. A. Reid, pp. 1-45.
   Presents biography of Williams and the early years of Providence. Emphasis on daily life in early years of town. Depends on materials from Arnold (1859.B1).

2 HILDRETH, RICHARD. <u>The History of the United States of America</u>. 2 vols. New York: Harper. I: 223, 305.
   Sees Williams as a traditional liberal democrat and considers this as the best way to understand his rebellion in the Massachusetts Bay Colony.

3 LODGE, HENRY C. "Review of Dexter's <u>As to Roger Williams</u>," <u>North American Magazine</u>, 73 (Oct.), 476-77.
   Finds Dexter's work (1876.A1) outstanding. Also points out that Williams's banishment was entirely justified and the only alternative for the Massachusetts Bay magistrates. Cites reasons for this conclusion.

1878 A BOOKS - NONE

1878 B SHORTER WRITINGS

1 L. A. R. "Roger Williams," <u>Phrenological Journal</u>, 65 (Nov.), 251-253.
   Examines problem of the early life of Williams and cites the fact that no information on his early years can be gained from his writings. Attempt to assemble information on his parents, place, and date of birth. Presents information from Cambridge University records suggesting that Williams may have attended there.

2 TYLER, MOSES COIT. <u>A History of American Literature, 1607-1765</u>. New York: George Putnam Sons. 2 vols. Reprinted, Ithaca: Cornell University Press, 1962, pp. 208-226.
   In-depth discussion and analysis of all of Williams's writings, especially the controversial writings between Williams and John Cotton. Compares Williams's writings on toleration with John Milton and finds Williams more eloquent and more noble. Of the <u>Bloudy Tenent Yet More Bloudy</u> he says, "here also are some of the best qualities that can be in a book: ripeness of judgment, uttermost sincerity, all consuming earnestness, the inspiration of being in the right and knowing it,...ample erudition, logic, imagination, noble emotion, humor, pathos, sarcasm,...torrents of eager and irresistible speech."

1879 A BOOKS - NONE

1879 B SHORTER WRITINGS

1 BURRAGE, HENRY S. "Concerning a Note in Dexter's As to Roger Williams," The Nation, 29 (25 Dec.), 436-37.
   Disputes accuracy of Dexter's treatment (1876.A1) of an incident where three Baptists visiting Massachusetts were persecuted by the magistrates. Williams sent a letter of protest and Burrage argues that Dexter plays down the severity of whipping inflicted on one of the members, Obadiah Holmes, in order to defend the magistrates' actions.

2 DEXTER, HENRY MARTYN. "Dr. Dexter and His Assailants," Nation, 29 (16 June), 433-34.
   Admits to possible error in reporting of Obadiah Holmes incident and resulting whipping as reported by Burrage in (1879.B1). Discusses role of Williams with magistrates. Defends the rest of his contentions in As to Roger Williams (1876.A1).

1880 A BOOKS

1 KING, HENRY MELVILLE. Early Baptists Defended. Boston: Howard Gannett, Publisher.
   Counter attack on those writers, especially among the Puritan historians, who failed to give proper credit to the pioneering efforts of early Baptists like Williams who tried to bring about religious toleration in Massachusetts and Rhode Island. Singles out Williams as important for the later development of religious liberty in America. Judges Williams was banished because of his Baptist views. Refutes Dexter's views in As to Roger Williams in treatment of Baptists (See 1876.A1).

1880 B SHORTER WRITINGS

1 BURRAGE, HENRY S. "Dexter's As to Roger Williams," The Nation, 30 (20 May), 384-385.
   Letter in answer to Dexter's refutation of attack on his book. Continues arguments on the role of Williams in writing to the Massachusetts Bay magistrates and Dexter's poor treatment of the events connected with it (See 1879.B2).

1881

1881 A BOOKS

1 DEXTER, HENRY MARTYN, ed. Christenings Make Not Christians. Rhode Island Historical Society Tracts No. 14. Providence: S. S. Rider.
   Brief introduction explains how tract was found and the background and origin of it. Summarizes main points.

1881 B SHORTER WRITINGS

1 RAE, W. F. "Founders of New England, Roger Williams," Good Words, 22: 786-792.
   Presentation of biography and analysis of various incidents associated with Williams's life in Boston, Salem, and Plymouth. Cites the reasons why Williams's banishment was wrong and the fact that the Massachusetts and New England of today is based on and cherishes his ideals of religious liberty.

2 WINSOR, J. "Bibliographical Note on Roger Williams," in The Memorial History of Boston. 4 vols. Boston: Ticknor and Co. I: 172-73.
   Brief treatment of banishment of Williams. Contains extensive bibliography of nineteenth-century writers on Williams.

1882 A BOOKS - NONE

1882 B SHORTER WRITINGS

1 BARTLETT, JOHN RUSSELL. "Roger Williams' Letters," The Literary World, 13 (12 Aug.), 259-260.
   Summarizes observations about letters assembled for The Writings of Roger Williams (1866.A1). Letters include 143 different numbers written mainly to friends and officials. The contents reflect many different aspects of Williams, the most important ones being the letters between Williams and Mrs. Sadleir.

2 DORR, HENRY C. The Planting and Growth of Providence. Rhode Island Historical Society Tracts, No. 15. Providence: S. S. Rider, pp. 1-45.
   Brief discussion in first part of book about Williams's role in the settling of early Providence. Examines his role as leader of the colonists.

3   RAE, W. F. "Roger Williams," Potter's American Monthly, 18: 209-215.
      Basic biography of Williams from the facts in Winthrop's Journal. Contains excerpts from the Bloudy Tenent. Discussion of charter and other events associated with early history of Rhode Island. Williams was a Baptist and then a Seeker. Williams was always ready to serve his fellow man.

1884 A BOOKS - NONE

1884 B SHORTER WRITINGS

1   DEANE, CHARLES. "Roger Williams," in Narrative and Critical History of America. Edited by Justin Winsor. Boston: Houghton Mifflin Company, p. 335.
      Disputes claims of earlier bographers of Williams that Massachusetts erred in its banishment of Williams. "Williams was banished from Massachusetts principally for political reasons. His peculiar opinions relating to soul liberty were not fully developed until after he had taken up his residence in Rhode Island....Williams here purchased, or received by gift a tract of land from the Indians, and he had no patent or other title to the soil...." Analyzes Williams's right to the land in Providence.

1885 A BOOKS - NONE

1885 B SHORTER WRITINGS

1   DORR, HENRY C. "The Narragansetts," Rhode Island Historical Society Collections, 7: 135-234.
      Extensive study of the Indians with several references to Williams's work with them.

1886 A BOOKS

1   ANON. Reunion of the Descendents of Roger Williams. Providence: June 22, n. p.
      Contains information and activities celebrating the reunion of Williams's descendents. Several speeches and other information about Williams and his deeds. Program of events at reunion dinner.

1886

2 GUILD, REUBEN ALDRIDGE. Footprints of Roger Williams. Providence: Tibbets & Preston.

　　Presents facts of Williams's life and the discovery of the apple tree root that had grown around Williams's skeleton. This discovery was made in 1860 when Williams's grave was opened. Discusses contributions made by Williams. Outlines main ideas in his writings. Discusses Welsh ancestry of Williams and plans to build a monument to his memory.

1886 B SHORTER WRITINGS

1 DURFEE, THOMAS. "An Oration on the 250th Anniversary of the Planting of Providence," in The Providence Plantation for Two Hundred and Fifty Years. Edited by Welcome Greene et al. Providence: J. A. and R. A. Reid, pp. 453-454.

　　Discussion of Williams's role in settling Providence and his concept of soul liberty. Sees soul liberty as the major contribution of Williams.

2 HOWLAND, JOHN ANDREWS. "The Date of Passing the Sentence of Banishment on Roger Williams," Rhode Island Historical Society Proceedings (1886-87), pp. 52-63.

　　Establishes date of the passing of sentence as October 9, 1635. Shows how this date has been confused in the past with Williams's date of departure from Salem. Also discusses the legend of Slate Rock, where Williams was supposed to have landed in Providence in 1636. Demonstrates there is no factual evidence to support story.

3 NOYES, ISAAC P. "Roger Williams," Phrenological Journal, 83: 64-65.

　　Sees Williams as a true moral hero whose life was a blessing to both his world and ours. Presents biography of Williams and sees him as both a statesman and moral reformer particularly in his concept of full and complete religious liberty and his charity toward the Indians.

4 RIDER, SIDNEY S. "The Wife of Roger Williams," Book Notes, 3 (13 March), 131.

　　Assembles all known information about Williams's wife. Incorrectly assumes her name to be Mary Warnard. Includes the dates of birth of her children and her kindnesses expressed in letters and gifts sent to Mrs. John Winthrop, etc.

1887 A BOOKS

1   GUILD, REUBEN ALDRIDGE. Second Paper on the Birth of Roger Williams. Providence: n.p.
    Examines evidence associated with Williams's birthplace and date. Presents latest findings about his probable date of birth.

1887 B SHORTER WRITINGS

1   ARMITAGE, THOMAS. A History of the Baptists. 2 vols. New York: Bryan & Taylor Company. I: 223, 305.
    Presents Williams as a religious hero in comparison with Christ. Williams "looms head and shoulders above his Puritan judges..." Discusses Williams as a member of the Baptist church and his pioneer work in America as well as Providence.

2   GUILD, REUBEN ALDRIDGE. "Roger Williams, Freeman of Massachusetts," Proceedings American Antiquarian Society, n.s., 5 (Oct.), 140-145.
    Presents details of Williams's taking of the freeman's oath in 1631 and the early colonial evidence of the event.

1888 A BOOKS - NONE

1888 B SHORTER WRITINGS

1   ANON. "The Authenticity of the Roger Williams' House," Historical Collections Essex Institute, 25: 162-64.
    Examines the evidence associated with Williams's house in Salem from the data available in old maps to determine the location and whether or not it was the parsonage.

2   GOODWIN, JOHN. The Pilgrim Republic, An Historical Review of the Colony of New Plymouth. Boston: Ticknor and Company, p. 348, ff.
    Summarizes a number of nineteenth-century reactions to Williams. Explains that his full idea of religious liberty was not developed until after reaching Providence. Goodwin sees a positive contribution in Williams's writings that was not accurately appreciated. Focus on activities of Williams at the Plymouth colony.

3   RIDER, SIDNEY S. "The Land Transaction Between Roger Williams and G. Bernon," Book Notes, 5 (17 Mar.), 29, 30.
    Disputes Knowles reference (1834.A1) to Williams's

1888

    (RIDER, SIDNEY S.)
        selling of land to one Gabriel Bernon. No evidence of this according to Rider who cites the fact that Bernon did not come to America until 1688, and that Bernon was not imprisoned prior to this. Knowles maintained that Williams's land sale was out of sympathy for Bernon.

4   WALL, CALEB. "Puritanism vs. The Quakers: Tributes to Roger Williams and William Penn," Proceedings American Antiquarian Society, n.s., 6.
        Demonstrates that Williams's colony for religious freedom in Rhode Island pre-dated William Penn's colony in Pennsylvania as the first colony of religious freedom in America.

1889 A BOOKS

1   RICHARDSON, ERASTUS. Roger Williams. Providence: n.p.
        Sub-titled "First Lecture in the Y. P. M. L. A. course" deals with the biography of Williams and the important contributions he made to religious liberty. Copy in Brown University Library.

1889 B SHORTER WRITINGS

1   AUSTIN, JOHN. Ancestry of Thirty-Three Rhode Islanders. Albany: Munsell's.
        Traces the descendents of Williams and other early settlers of Rhode Island for five generations. Lists children of Williams as: Mary, Joseph, Freeborn, Providence, Mercy, and Daniel. Contains genealogy charts on Williams and others.

2   LOWNDES, G. A. "Letters of Roger Williams to Lady Barrington," New England Historical and Genealogical Register, 43 (July), 315-20.
        Presents newly discovered letter from Williams to Lady Barrington discussing Williams's plans for marriage. Also fills in background information about Williams's life prior to coming to America.

3   WATERS, HENRY F. "Genealogical Gleanings in England," New England Historical and Genealogical Register, 43: 291-93, 294-303.
        Concerned with the discovery in England of the will of James Williams, the father of Williams. Details of will are presented. Also in Waters' book, Genealogical Gleanings in England. 2 vols.

1890 A BOOKS - NONE

1890 B SHORTER WRITINGS

1   BANNING, H. E. "The Story of Roger Williams Retold," Magazine of American History, 24 (Oct.), 314, 318.
    Biographical portrait of Williams citing his contributions to American democracy. Also refers to him as a "prolific writer" and includes a list of his writings with a brief discussion of each.

1891 A BOOKS

1   ALLEN, W. F. "The Case of Roger Williams," Unitarian Review, 35: 20-33.
    Takes exception to (1876.A1) assertion that Williams's religious belief had nothing to do with his banishment. "The real ground for the banishment of Roger Williams was the same as in the case of Ann Hutchinson, the Quakers, and the Anabaptists,--as disturbers of the community." Reviews the evidence in letters and records about Williams's trial etc. Williams's banishment helped temper his spirit and his nature.

2   ELLIS, GEORGE E. The Puritan Age and Rule in the Colony of Massachusetts Bay, 1629-1685. Boston: Houghton Mifflin, Chapter 8.
    Devotes an entire chapter to the banishment of Williams. Blames Williams for the troubles that Ellis sees were brought on by himself. Biography and background of the major incidents in Williams's life.

3   RIDER, SIDNEY S. "The Political Results of the Banishment of Williams," Book Notes, 8 (15 Aug.), 129-33.
    What has not been observed before is the political advantage that Massachusetts enjoyed because of Williams's banishment. Williams saved Massachusetts from destruction by the Indians in relation to the Pequot tribe. Map shows locations of major tribes and how Williams averted trouble several times. Points out that even though Hubbard was aware of Williams's vital role, Hubbard said nothing about Williams's help in (1680.B1) nor of the important role Williams played in Pequot affair.

1891 B SHORTER WRITINGS

1   RIDER, SIDNEY S. "An Inquiry Concerning An Alleged Portrait of Roger Williams," Rhode Island Historical Society Tracts,

1891

(RIDER, SIDNEY S.)
Second Series, No. 2.
Demonstrates that there are no portraits of Williams, only word descriptions, which Rider assembles in this article.

1892 A BOOKS

1   ELY, W. D. *A Keyhole for Roger Williams' Key, or a Study of Suggested Misprints in Its Sixteenth Chapter*. Providence: Standard Printing Company.
In this paper read before the Rhode Island Historical Society, Ely argues that the word <u>barnes</u> is incorrect in the edition of *A Key* published by the society. The correct word should be <u>beanes</u>. Offers contextual evidence to support his position.

2   GUILD, REUBEN ALDRIDGE. *Roger Williams, The Pioneer Missionary to the Indians*. Philadelphia: n.p.
Examines Williams's early work with the Indians in contrast with the work of the Puritan missionary, John Eliot. Reprinted in *Baptist Home Mission Monthly*, 14: 325-31.

3   MERRIMAN, TITUS. *The Pilgrims, Puritans, and Roger Williams Vindicated: and His Sentence of Banishment Ought to be Revoked*. Boston: Bradley & Woodruff.
Merriman led a movement to revoke the banishment against Williams in 1901. This book details his reasons for it. Part I is devoted to a discussion of the background of Williams and his ideas of religious liberty. Part II presents reasons for revoking the banishment. He compares Williams and Christ as teaching the same doctrines. Next, Williams's work was ultimately successful and both Puritans and Williams had equal rights. Finally, he suggests Massachusetts ought to build a monument to Williams to make amends for past errors.

1892 B SHORTER WRITINGS

1   CAMPBELL, DOUGLAS. *The Puritans in Holland, England, and America*. 2 vols. New York: Harper and Brothers. II: 204.
Salutes Williams's teaching that the conscience should be free but says that the Bay magistrates banished him as a menace to public order and that only twenty-three years before, "the mother country had burned Edward Wightman at the stake for the same religious opinions." Attacks Williams because of his weakening of the colony of Massachusetts Bay.

1894

2 NEWMAN, A. H. "Roger Williams," Magazine of Christian Literature, 5, no. 4, pp. 271-282.
Defends Williams as the founder of the first Baptist church in America. Examines details of founding of church in Rhode Island. Shows Williams carrying out principles of Baptist belief in colony at Providence. Williams also accomplished scholar.

1893 A BOOKS - NONE

1893 B SHORTER WRITINGS

1 STRAUS, OSCAR. "Roger Williams and John Cotton," Author's Club Liber Scriptorum First Book. New York: The Author's Club.
Compares the liberal ideas of both Cotton and Williams. Finds that Cotton "lacked the moral courage to defend principles against power," while Williams stood up for his belief in religious liberty.

2 WATERS, HENRY F. "Genealogy of Roger Williams," New England Historical and Genealogical Register, 47: 498-99.
Discussion of Williams's family history tracing lines back from father James Williams. (See also 1899.B2.)

1894 A BOOKS

1 STRAUS, OSCAR. Roger Williams: The Pioneer of Religious Liberty. New York: Century.
Biography based in part on Knowles (1834.A1) and others. Discusses the significance of Williams's actions to the future course of history. Examines the roles of Gorton and Hutchinson and their relationship to the suffering and banishment Williams endured. Concludes Williams "not only saw far in advance of his own day but had the fortitude and holy determination, single handed, to combat the overwhelming spirit of fanaticism and bigotry of his generation and to suffer martyrdom for a principle which has steadily been making progress in the circuit of the globe and to which we owe the chief blessings that flow from an enlightened age."

1894 B SHORTER WRITINGS

1 ANON. "Roger Williams, The Pioneer of Religious Liberty," Book Notes, 11: 145-150.

1894

    (ANON.)
        Review of Straus' book on Williams (1894.A1). Takes exception to treatment of some details of Williams's journey to Rhode Island. Contains useful survey of nineteenth-century treatments of Roger Williams.

2 ELY, W. D. "Roger Williams' *Key*: Beanes vs. Barnes," *Rhode Island Historical Society Publications*, 2: 189-196.
    Further development of argument for change in words *beanes* for *barnes* as they occur in society's edition of Williams's *Key*.

3 NEWMAN, A. H. *A History of the Baptist Churches in the United States*. New York, pp. 59-96.
    Argues that Williams was a Baptist both before and after his banishment and that in order to understand him it is necessary to understand his Baptist principles. Shows how Williams founded first Baptist church in America.

4 RIDER, SIDNEY S. "The Repeal of the Decree of Banishment against Roger Williams in 1676," *Book Notes*, 11: 217-219.
    Cites act of Massachusetts Council in March 31, 1676, allowing Williams to return to Bay colony if he would leave his religion behind in Rhode Island. Evidence that Williams was banished for religious reasons. Refutes arguments of Dexter (1876.A1) and Vose (1894.B6).

5 TOOKER, WILLIAM WALLACE. "Roger Williams Vindicated: or An Answer to 'A Keyhole for Roger Williams' *Key*," *Rhode Island Historical Society Publications*, 2: 61-67.
    An answer to Ely's article (1894.B1) on the misprint of the word *barnes* for *beanes* in Chapter Sixteen of Williams's *Key*. Argues that the text is correct with the word *barnes*.

6 _____. "The *Key*: Fact versus Theory," *Rhode Island Historical Society Publications*, 2: 237-41.
    Further develops argument of previous article showing that Ely's theory (1894.B1) is wrong on the question of word misprints.

7 VOSE, JAMES G. "A Note on the Transaction of Roger Williams and others in Selling Indians into Slavery," *Rhode Island Historical Society Publications*, 1: 239-240.
    Points out that Williams was not against selling into slavery prisoners taken during war time. Cites evidence of three Indians sold in 1678 in Sandwich. Evidence in Vol. I, Foster Collection in the Rhode Island Historical Society Library.

8   WALKER, W. "Roger Williams," <u>Nation</u>, 59: 35.
     Presents review of Dexter's book (1876.A1) and examines the facts associated with Williams's banishment.

1895 A BOOKS - NONE

1895 B SHORTER WRITINGS

1   ARNOLD, FRED AUGUSTUS. "Note on Roger Williams' Statue," <u>Rhode Island Historical Society Publications</u>, 3: 127.
     Cites irony of Williams's statue and painting depicting him with long hair as Chapter 7, p. 58 of <u>A Key</u> presents his very strong views against such long hair on men.

2   DORR, HENRY C. "The Initial Deed From Roger Williams of the Land Purchased of Canonicus and Meantonnonmi," <u>Rhode Island Historical Society Publications</u>, 3: 155-58.
     Discusses the terms of the deed drawn up between Williams and the Indians. Explains Williams's point about his concern for paying the Indians for the land.

1896 A BOOKS

1   KING, HENRY MELVILLE. <u>A Summer Visit of Three Rhode Islanders to the Massachusetts Bay in 1651</u>. Providence: Preston and Rounds.
     Explains the visit of three Baptists from Rhode Island to Lynn, Massachusetts, and the resulting punishment of one of them, Obadiah Holmes by whipping. Includes Williams's letter of protest sent to the Bay magistrates about the treatment of Holmes. Refutes Dexter's treatment (1876.A1) of the issue.

2   PAINE, GEORGE T. <u>A Denial of the Charges of Forgery in Connection with Sachems' Deed to Roger Williams</u>. Providence: Standard Printing.
     Contains photos of original deed and explains William Harris's role of part of the deed as well as Williams.

3   RIDER, SIDNEY S. <u>The Forgeries Connected With The Deed Given by the Sachems Canonicus and Miantonomi to Roger Williams</u>. Providence: <u>Rhode Island Historical Society Tracts, Second Series, No. 4</u>.
     Discusses the unsuccessful attempt of William Harris to alter Williams's original deed to Providence. Attempted forgeries occurred in 1658 and had nothing to do with Williams. Lengthy discussion of Harris's role.

1896

4   WHITSETT, WILLIAM H. A Question in Baptist History: The Baptism of Roger Williams. Louisville: C. T. Dearing.
    Argues that Williams was baptized by sprinkling rather than by the usual method of immersion. Whitsett was President of the Southern Baptist Theological Seminary. (See also 1897.A4.)

1896 B SHORTER WRITINGS

1   BROOKS, MRS. HENRY. "Roger Williams in Salem," Essex Institute Bulletin, 28: 77-86.
    Examines Williams's life in Salem and what he did there that foreshadowed the eventual break with the Bay magistrates. Sees Williams as an heroic figure even before the famous banishment.

2   DEAN, J. W. "Early Statements Relative to the Early Life of Roger Williams," New England Historical and Genealogical Register, 50: 169-171.
    Refers to statements by Ezekiel Rogers and Jane Whalley relative to the early life of Williams. Information is from letters by Williams to Lady Barrington.

3   EGGLESTON, EDWARD. "Roger Williams: The Prophet of Religious Freedom," in Library of the World's Best Literature. Edited by Charles D. Warner. New York: Peale and Bill. Vol. 13: 5219-5224
    Detailed life of Williams and a study of his banishment from the Massachusetts Bay. Regards Williams as a noble spirit far in advance of his age and looks at the banishment as a clear attempt at persecution for religious beliefs. Presents running series of marginal glosses documenting the sources of his information and conclusions, showing original sources that he used in his evaluation of Williams.

4   RIDER, SIDNEY S. "The Alleged Baptism of Roger Williams by Holliman," Book Notes, 13: 121-125.
    Cites fact that no evidence exists on either Williams's or Holliman's part that Williams was ever baptized at all. The concern for Williams's baptism came from later Massachusetts writers and Rhode Island Baptists. Examines statements of Winthrop, Morton, and Hubbard on the subject of the baptism.

1897 A BOOKS

1   AUSTIN, JOHN C. Roger Williams Calendar. Central Falls: Freeman.
    A selection of Williams's writings for each day of the year.

2   _____. Index to Subjects in the Roger Williams Calendar. Providence. Privately printed.
    Pamphlet that lists the subject matter of selections in 1897.A1 as well as an index to names of persons.

3   BUTTERWORTH, HEZEKIAH. In the Days of Massasoit, A Tale of Roger Williams. Philadelphia: Baptist Publication Society.
    Fictional tale of Williams and Indians illustrating his friendship with them. Combines fact with fictional recreation.

4   KING, HENRY MELVILLE. The Baptism of Roger Williams. Providence: Preston and Rounds.
    Refutes Dr. William Whitsett's contention (1896.A1) that Williams was baptized by sprinkling rather than immersion. King argues that Williams was a traditional Baptist baptized in the regular way of immersion. Focus on the role Williams played in setting up the first Baptist church in America. Concludes, "Any man who has made himself familiar with the life of Roger Williams, and has studied his character, and estimated his achievements will feel that such a treatment [Whitsett's] of him shows an utter failure to appreciate the man whose principles of civil and religious liberty courageously proclaimed and successfully illustrated, have been the supreme moulding influence in making this nation what it is."

5   RIDER, SIDNEY S. Soul Liberty, Rhode Island's Gift to the Nation. Providence: S. S. Rider.
    Argues that Williams and Rhode Island were the first responsible for religious liberty in American and denies the claims of writers that say that Lord Baltimore and Maryland have first claim to these honors. Cites evidence and dates to support.

1897 B SHORTER WRITINGS

1   EGGLESTON, EDWARD. The Beginners of A Nation, A History of the Source and Rise of the Earliest English Settlements

1897

(EGGLESTON, EDWARD)
in America With Special Reference to the Life and Character of the People. New York: D. Appleton. Book 3, Chapter 2.
Contains a detailed life of Williams and his banishment from Massachusetts. Reprinted from 1896.B3.

1898 A BOOKS - NONE

1898 B SHORTER WRITINGS

1   FISKE, JOHN. The Beginnings of New England, or The Puritan Theocracy in Its Relation to Civil and Religious Liberty. Boston: Houghton Mifflin, pp. 114-116, 151-158, 184-186.
    Sees Williams as a gentle and kindly soul much in advance of his age amongst the Puritans. He deals with Williams in the course of his history, especially in relation to Williams's work with the Indians.

1899 A BOOKS - NONE

1899 B SHORTER WRITINGS

1   BURRAGE, HENRY S. "Review of Dexter's As to Roger Williams," American Historical Association Report, 1: 10-12.
    A negative review of Dexter's book (1876.A1) citing the importance of Baptist beliefs and teachings in Williams's life and the persecution charges against Massachusetts. Points out that Dexter has not presented the facts correctly about Williams.

2   FISKE, JOHN. A History of the United States For Schools. Boston: Houghton Mifflin.
    Contains essentially the same information as (1898.B1) with an added emphasis on the heroic aspects of Williams's deeds. Sees Williams as gentle and kindly soul.

3   HODGES, ALMON DANFORTH. "Notes Concerning Roger Williams," New England Historical and Genealogical Register, 53: 60-64.
    Adds four pieces of information about Williams: (1) date of birth 1604, (2) date of death April 1683, (3) wife's maiden name Warnard, (4) corrects letter in Backus History (See 1777.B1) from Williams to Hubbard.

1900 A BOOKS

1   TRUMBULL, ANNIE ELIOT. *Mistress Content Cradock*. New York: Barnes and Noble.
    Fictional tale in which Williams is a central character.

1900 B SHORTER WRITINGS

1   AMES, CHARLES GORDON. "Roger Williams," in *Prophets of Liberalism*. Boston: West Publishers, pp. 7-15.
    Suggests that Williams found his place among Baptists and that we can learn from his example to avoid spiritual tyranny in our age. Williams "was not impeached for heresy, but for schism; and schism was identical with anarchy."

2   BRIGHAM, C. S. "Roger Williams' Wife," *Rhode Island Historical Society Publications*, n.s., 8: 67-68.
    Corrects earlier misconception that Mary Barnard was the maiden name of Williams's wife (See 1899.B3).

3   HODGES, ALMON DANFORTH. "Note Concerning Roger Williams," *New England Historical and Genealogical Register*, 54: 212.
    Changes earlier article information in 1899.B3 of Williams's wife's maiden name from Warnard to Barnard.

4   MATTHEWS, ALBERT R. "Roger Williams and Sir Thomas Urquhart," *Nation*, 70: 435-36.
    Cites reference to Williams's aid offered to Urquhart who was imprisoned in Windsor Castle. Williams was instrumental in Urquhart's release and Matthews speculates event must have happened between November 1651 and February 1653.

5   SECCOMBE, T. "Roger Williams," in *Dictionary of National Biography*, Vol. 61: 445-450.
    Contains a brief biography of Williams. Also contains a bibliography of writings about Williams.

1901 A BOOKS

1   HALL, RUTH. *The Golden Arrow: A Story of Roger Williams Day*. Boston: Houghton Mifflin.
    Novel for young children with Williams as a hero.

1901 B SHORTER WRITINGS

1   BURRAGE, HENRY S. "Why was Roger Williams Banished?" *American Journal of Theology*, 5 (Jan.), 1-17.

Roger Williams: A Reference Guide

1901

    (BURRAGE, HENRY S.)
        A detailed discussion of the four points of dispute Williams raised with the magistrates. Burrage rejects the conclusion of Dexter (See 1876.A1) and states that "most clearly and unmistakably" Williams's doctrine of soul liberty was the basis of the banishment.

1902 A BOOKS - NONE

1902 B SHORTER WRITINGS

1   BRIGHAM, C. S. "Gift of Compass of Roger Williams," Rhode Island Historical Society Proceedings (1902-03), 32-33.
        Deals with presentation of compass to Society and the authenticity of it. Given by Mrs. John Carter Brown.

2   _____. Bibliography of Rhode Island History. Boston and Syracuse: Mason Publishing Company, pp. 680-681.
        Contains a bibliography of Williams dealing mainly with nineteenth-century journal articles as well as the major biographies. No annotations.

3   CARPENTER, EDMUND J. "Roger Williams and the Plantation at Providence," New England Magazine, n.s., 26 (May), 353-364.
        Attempt to clear away some of the "rubbish" that surrounds Williams's name. States that Williams, like all great leaders, was without doubt erratic at times. If not the greatest certainly most progressive of the Puritans.

1903 A BOOKS - NONE

1903 B SHORTER WRITINGS

1   FAUNCE, W. H. PERRY. "Roger Williams and his Doctrine of Soul Liberty," in Pioneers of Religious Liberty in America. Boston: American Unitarian Association, pp. 47-82.
        Discusses the treatment of Williams at the hands of Palfrey (1858.B2), Dexter (1876.A1), and Lodge (1877.B3), pointing out the error of failing to understand Williams's soul liberty as the focal point of his thought.

2   JOHNSON, LUCIAN. "Religious Liberty in Maryland and Rhode Island," Brooklyn: International Catholic Truth Society, pp. 19-47.
        Asserts that neither Rhode Island nor Maryland have the first claim for the founding of religious freedom, that

1904

religious liberty was not pioneered by Williams but goes back much further to the history of the early Church. Presents background data.

3   KING, HENRY MELVILLE. Religious Liberty. Providence: Preston and Rounds, pp. 70-124.
    Extensive analysis of the history of the movement for religious liberty with particular attention to Williams's role. Focuses on his contributions and principles at his trial.

4   KOHLER, MAX J. "Phases in the History of Religious Liberty in America with Special Reference to the Jews," American Jewish Historical Society Publications, 11: 53-73.
    Broad survey of toleration of Jews in America citing Williams's granting of freedom as earliest example.

5   MERRIMAN, TITUS M. "America's Debt To Roger Williams," National Magazine, 17: 623-627.
    Summary of the reasons why Williams's decree of banishment should be lifted and a monument erected to him in Boston. Presents Williams's biography and the various attempts through the years to revoke the sentence of banishment on such a great person.

1904 A BOOKS - NONE

1904 B SHORTER WRITINGS

1   OSGOOD, HERBERT L. The American Colonies in the Seventeenth Century. 2 vols. New York: Macmillan Company. I, Chapter 7.
    Discusses the history of Rhode Island and Williams. Concerned with Williams's role in securing the initial deed and later the charter for the Providence Plantation. Sees Williams as important for these areas as well as his concern with religious liberty.

2   RIDER, SIDNEY S. The Lands of Rhode Island As They Were Known to Cannounicus and Miantonnomu When Roger Williams Came in 1636. Providence: S. S. Rider, pp. 1-25.
    Contains a discussion of the Indian characteristics as noted in Williams's A Key. Examines the forgeries connected with the deed originally given to Williams.

3   _____. "In Defence of Rhode Island as Founded By Roger Williams," Book Notes, 21 (3 Dec.), 193-215.

1904

> (RIDER, SIDNEY S.)
> Criticizes treatment of Williams by Osgood in 1904.B1, claiming that proper attention was not given to Williams's importance. The founding of Rhode Island "was an event greater than the foundation of Greece or Rome and second only to Palestine." (See 1904.B1.)

1907 A BOOKS

1   KING, HENRY MELVILLE. The True Roger Williams. An Address Delivered at the First Baptist Meeting House, Providence, Rhode Island. Providence: Townsend, July 28.
    Argues that in order to understand Williams one must appreciate his role as a Baptist minister in seventeenth-century Rhode Island. Examines Williams's ideas and writings that relate to the traditional Baptist beliefs of the period. Shows how his ideas of soul liberty are in conformity with them.

2   NOYES, ISAAC P. Dramatic Poem: Roger Williams and Soul Liberty, Washington, D. C., n.p.
    Poem about Williams and his contribution of soul liberty as main theme. Contains seven pages. Copy in Brown University Library.

1907 B SHORTER WRITINGS

1   COLCORD, W. A. "What Were the Principles for Which Roger Williams Was Banished?" Liberty, 2, No. 4, 19-21.
    Argues that Williams's democratic principles were the basis for his banishment from the Massachusetts Bay Colony.

1908 A BOOKS

1   EATON, AMASA. Roger Williams: The Founder of Providence--The Pioneer of Religious Liberty. Providence: Department of Education.
    This booklet, designed for public schools, relates the essential facts about his life. Also surveys the opinions of Williams from Mather down to the period of the Knowles (1834.A1) and Elton (1853.A1) biographies.

2   RICHMAN, IRVING B. Rhode Island, Its Making and Meaning. New York: G. P. Putnam's Sons. 2 vols.
    Deals with the period 1636-1683. Examines Williams's role in setting up the colony. Presents early history and incidents involved in Williams's administration of government. Includes maps.

1908 B SHORTER WRITINGS

1   CARPENTER, EDMUND J. "The Strange Story of Roger Williams," Grafton Magazine, 1: 18-25.
    Examines evidence about Williams revealed in letter to Lady Barrington and the relationship between Williams and Jane Whalley. Suggests that Williams was more aware of Separatist position in England than in Massachusetts. Relates events in Plymouth and Salem.

2   HOSMER, JAMES K., ed. History of New England, 1630-1649, by John Winthrop. Original Narratives Series. New York: Charles Scribner's.
    Another edition of Winthrop's Journal useful for its full annotations and index (See 1649.B1). I: 61-62, 116-117, 162-163, 168, 184-185, 187-189, 218, 221, 272. II: 7, 96, 350.

3   KING, HENRY MELVILLE. "Roger Williams and the Pilgrims," Nation, 86 (7 May), 421-422.
    Suggests that a recent book by Frederick A Noble, The Pilgrims, does not correctly represent Williams as the liberal person that he was. Disputes several issues about Williams, particularly treatment of Quakers by Williams.

1909 A BOOKS

1   CARPENTER, EDMUND J. Roger Williams: A Study of the Life, Times, and Character of a Political Pioneer. New York: Grafton Press.
    Relates Williams to the political and religious movements of his time. Emphasis on understanding the early life of Williams in England and his strong association with the Separatist movement. Sees issue of banishment of Williams as primarily a political decision forced on the magistrates as a result of Williams's actions. Offers several letters from Winthrop, Cotton, Lady Barrington, Mrs. Sadleir, and Vane in support of his argument about Williams. Finally concludes with discussion of both the strengths and weaknesses of Williams.

2   KING, HENRY MELVILLE. Sir Henry Vane Jr. Governor of Massachusetts, and Friend of Roger Williams. Providence: Preston and Rounds.
    Booklet deals with the relationship between Williams and Vane and the strong feelings Vane had against the Bay for banishing Williams.

1909

    3   MOWRY, WILLIAM A. Concerning Roger Williams: An Address. Pamphlet in Rhode Island Historical Society Library. Providence: n.p.
          Address delivered before Hyde Park Historical Society, Oct. 25. Points out the conscientious and independent spirit of Williams in his ideas of government and his concern for Indians. Cites Carpenter (1909.A1) as the main source of his ideas.

1909 B SHORTER WRITINGS

    1   KING, HENRY MELVILLE. "John Calvin and Roger Williams," The Baptist World (30 Sept.), p. 3.
          Reports on the events surrounding the dedication of the statue of Williams in Geneva in the summer of 1909. Remarks by Dr. Charles Gorgeaud explain the importance of Williams to the idea of freedom of religion not only in America but around the world.

1910 A BOOKS - NONE

1910 B SHORTER WRITINGS

    1   DROWNE, HENRY RUSSELL. "Heirlooms of the First Americans," Journal of American History, 4, No. 3. 425-28.
          Deals with discovery of Williams's watch and its presentation to Rhode Island Historical Society.

1912 A BOOKS

    1   LEIGHTON, ETTA VERONICA. The Story of Roger Williams and the Founding of Rhode Island. Dansville, New York: F. A. Owen Publishing Company.
          Booklet designed for public schools. Contains biography, ideas in his writings and photographs of monuments to Williams.

    2   SIMON, ABRAM. The Prophet of Soul Liberty, A Sunday Discourse Before the Reform Congregational Kenseath, Israel, of Philadelphia. Philadelphia: n.p.
          An address that focuses on Williams's idea of toleration and soul liberty. Discusses his policy of tolerance of Jews in both England and America. Need for Williams today.

1912 B SHORTER WRITINGS

1   KIMBALL, GERTRUDE S. Providence in Colonial Times. Boston: Houghton Mifflin, pp. 3-144.
    Brief discussion and biography dealing with Williams's role in governing early Providence. Contains maps and sketches of early Providence.

2   RIDER, SIDNEY S. "The Ancestry of Roger Williams," Book Notes, 29, no. 11 (25 May), 65-67, no. 12 (8 June), 89-93.
    Disputes Moriarity (1913.B1) on the accurate knowledge of Williams's ancestry by two legal documents. Evidence cited is in a 1644 Chancery case brought by Sidrack Williams against Williams.

1913 A BOOKS - NONE

1913 B SHORTER WRITINGS

1   MORIARITY, G. A. Jr. "The Ancestry of Roger Williams," New England Historical and Genealogical Register, 67: 90-91.
    Points out that the above information in Book Notes by Rider (1912.B2) is nothing new and had been suggested twenty-three years earlier by H. Waters (See 1889.B2). Concerns suit in Chancery of Williams's brother. Also concludes that Williams was son of James and Alice Williams.

1916 A BOOKS

1   CHAPIN, HOWARD MILLAR. Documentary History of Rhode Island. 2 vols. Providence: Preston and Rounds.
    Presents Williams's deed and other documents connected with the founding and early settlement and administration of Providence. Presents photo of deed, Vol. 2, p. 26.

1916 B SHORTER WRITINGS

1   PAGE, SAMUEL DAVIS. "Roger Williams, President of Rhode Island," Pennsylvania Society of Colonial Governors Transactions, 1: 184-206.
    Paper read by one of the descendents of Williams dealing with Williams's leadership role in Providence. Most of material is derived from Straus (1894.A1). Specific discussion of Williams as president of Rhode Island covers the period 1654-1657.

1916

2   PERLEY, SIDNEY. "Where Roger Williams Lived in Salem," <u>Essex Institute Historical Collections</u>, 52: 97-111.
    Takes issue with the legend that Williams lived in the first house built in Salem. Demonstrates that house in question was owned by William Williams who came to Salem in 1637. With the aid of maps Perley establishes the fact that Williams's house was sold to Higginson prior to his departure to Rhode Island.

1917 A BOOKS

1   HALL, MAY EMERY. <u>Roger Williams</u>. Boston: Pilgrim Press.
    Popular biography of Williams combining historical fact with speculative conversations on what Williams might have thought and said in various circumstances of his life. Presents Williams as a character of heroic stature.

2   KING, HENRY MELVILLE. <u>John Eliot and Roger Williams</u>. Providence: Mayes Printing Company.
    This pamphlet suggests that the contributions of Williams in the areas of religious liberty, separation of church and state, and the role of government have overshadowed his famous work amongst the Indians. Finds Williams's work with Indians to be of much more lasting value than Eliot's. Uses several passages from <u>A Key</u> to demonstrate why Williams deserves the title "Apostle to the Indians" as much as Eliot does. Reprinted in <u>Review and Expositor</u>, 14, no. 3, July.

1917 B SHORTER WRITINGS - NONE

1918 A BOOKS

1   BICKNELL, THOMAS W. <u>Roger Williams, Not Founder of Rhode Island</u>. Pamphlet, Rhode Island Historical Society Library, n.p., c. 1918.
    Contends that the founders of Aquidneck Island were first to discover what is now known as Rhode Island. This was before Williams had discovered Providence. Offers evidence in support of thesis.

2   CHAPIN, HOWARD MILLAR. <u>Report on the Burial Place of Roger Williams</u>. Providence: Rhode Island Historical Society.
    Assembles the evidence regarding the burial place of Williams and concludes that Williams was buried near his house in Providence. Contains maps and other useful material about the death of Williams.

3   ____. *A List of Roger Williams' Writings*. Providence: Preston and Rounds.
     A useful listing of all of Williams's writings, unpublished at the time of his death, including dates of composition, the various printings, and location of originals.

1918 B SHORTER WRITINGS

1   ANON. "Roger Williams' Wife," *Rhode Island Historical Society Collections*, 11 (Oct.), 122-124.
     Letter of Lady Masham identifies Williams's wife as Mary Barnard and announces her forthcoming marriage. Letter was recently discovered in England.

2   BICKNELL, THOMAS W. "Rhode Island: Boston the Preparatory School for Aquidneck," *Americana*, 12 (July), 319-342.
     Account of the circumstances in the Massachusetts Bay Colony that brought about the banishment of Williams and the founding of Rhode Island.

3   CHAPIN, HOWARD MILLAR. "List of Roger Williams' Writings," *Rhode Island Historical Society Collections*, 11: 11-17.
     Reprint of 1917.B3.

1919 A BOOKS

1   STRICKLAND, ARTHUR B. *Roger Williams, Prophet and Pioneer of Soul-Liberty*. Boston: Judson Press.
     Cites Williams as an example of patriotic hero needed after World War as an inspiration and example of those who took a stand when religious liberty was threatened in the past. Deals with Williams's biography and accentuates those areas that show the best in American life. Includes a detailed walking tour of the landmarks of Providence associated with Williams. Focus on Williams's concept of soul liberty and its meaning today.

2   STRAUS, OSCAR. *The Prophet of Liberty, Address delivered at Madison Avenue Baptist Church, New York, January 13*. New York: n.p.
     An expansion of Straus' ideas in biography of Williams (1894.A1), on the concept of soul liberty and its importance to America.

1919

1919 B SHORTER WRITINGS

1   MORRIS, CHARLES. <u>Heroes of Progress in America</u>. 2nd edition. Philadelphia: J. B. Lippincott. Chapter 1.
    Contains a biography of Williams and explains his contribution to progress in the freedom of religion.

1920 A BOOKS – NONE

1920 B SHORTER WRITINGS

1   EAGER, GEORGE B. "Calvin and Roger Williams in Relation to Religious Liberty," <u>Review and Expositor</u>, 17, no. 3 (July), 341-48.
    Suggests comparison between Calvin and Williams as advocates of religious liberty. Calvin believed in liberty and Williams carried forth the idea to its completion. Quotes from Straus (1894.A1), Richman (1908.A2), Bancroft (1843.B1) and others to show how Williams was the first to popularize the idea. At this point in time (1920) we are more aware than ever of Williams's contribution.

2   PETERSON, FRANK. "Roger Williams, The Contender for Soul Liberty," <u>Midwinter, Böken for 1920</u>, pp. 27-36.
    Presents biography of Williams with special attention to his founding of Providence and contributions to religious freedom. Also points out the graves of Williams and his wife and relates Williams to the founding of the Baptist Church in America in 1639.

3   POTTER, GEORGE R. "Roger Williams and John Milton," <u>Rhode Island Historical Society Collections</u>, 13 (Oct.), 113-129.
    Examines evidence of the relationship between Milton and Williams and the fact that Williams helped Milton to learn Dutch. (<u>See also</u> 1859.B1.)

1921 A BOOKS – NONE

1921 B SHORTER WRITINGS

1   ANON. "Roger Williams Tablet in the Hall of Fame," <u>Rhode Island Historical Society Collections</u>, 14 (July), 65-67.
    Presents information on the tablet and inscription about Williams in the Hall of Fame of Great Americans at New York University.

Roger Williams: A Reference Guide

1924

2   CREEL, GEORGE. Sons of the Eagle: Soaring Figures From America's Past. Indianapolis: Bobbs Merrill.
    Account of Williams's life and deeds focusing on his suffering at the hands of cruel Puritans of Massachusetts.

3   MORRIS, RICHARD B. "The Jewish Interests of Roger Williams," The American Hebrew, 110 (9 Dec.), 132-138, 141-147.
    Focuses on Williams's concept of toleration of all religious sects and his concern for toleration of Jews in both England and Providence. Cites Williams's use of Old Testament in his writings with his most direct knowledge of Hebrew in Christenings Make Not Christians. Also concerned with origins of Jews in Rhode Island.

1922 A BOOKS - NONE

1922 B SHORTER WRITINGS

1   CHRISTIAN, JOHN T. A History of the Baptists of the United States. Nashville: Broadman Press, pp. 365-375.
    Identifies the type of baptism given to Williams and refers to him as the first Baptist preacher in America. Contends the Baptists of America did not derive their origin from Williams but rather from the churches in England and Wales.

1923 A BOOKS - NONE

1923 B SHORTER WRITINGS

1   CHAPIN, HOWARD MILLAR. "Early Life of Roger Williams," Rhode Island Historical Society Collections, 16: 78-83.
    Summarizes most recent findings on the early life of Williams in England. Explains Williams's contact with Masham, Lady Barrington, and Jane Whalley. Includes photographs of English places associated with Williams like Cambridge, Pembroke College, etc.

1924 A BOOKS

1   CHAPIN, HOWARD MILLAR, ed. Letters and Papers of Roger Williams, 1629-1682, Boston: Massachusetts Historical Society.
    Brief introduction and description of a group of ten letters omitted from The Writings of Roger Williams,

Roger Williams: A Reference Guide

1924

(CHAPIN, HOWARD MILLAR)
(1866.A1) 1866-74. Letters are photo copies and contain several complete versions of "cut" copies of letters in The Writings.

1924 B SHORTER WRITINGS

1   COWELL, HENRY J. "George Fox and Roger Williams: A Battle of Giants," The Baptist Quarterly, n.s., 2: 132-136.
    Discusses how close Williams and Fox came to debating in 1672 and how Williams debated with William Edmundson instead. Presents the arguments of both Williams and Edmundson and comments on the observations about the debates. Refers to the real battle between Williams and Fox in the books each later wrote.

1925 A BOOKS - NONE

1925 B SHORTER WRITINGS

1   ISHAM, NORMAN M. "The House of Roger Williams," Rhode Island Historical Society Collections, 18 (Apr.), 33-39.
    Report on the excavations made in 1906 of the location of Williams's house in Providence, near North Main Street. Includes several photographs and concludes house was 1-1/2 story with a shallow foundation. Excavation was made by Isham.

2   STEWART, WALTER SINCLAIR. "Roger Williams" in Early Baptist Missionaries and Pioneers. Boston: The Judson Press, pp. 17-43.
    Contains biography and study of Williams's ideas and Baptist principles. Sees these as basis for religious liberty. Discusses baptism in 1639 and founding of first Baptist church in America.

1926 A BOOKS - NONE

1926 B SHORTER WRITINGS

1   CHRISTIAN, JOHN T. A History of the Baptists of the United States From the First Settlement of the Country to the Year 1845. Nashville: Broadman Press, pp. 38-40.
    This work argues that "so far as is known not one Baptist Church or minister came out of the Providence Church of this period or was in any wise affected by the baptism of Roger Williams." Focuses generally on Williams as a Baptist and his life in Providence.

1927

2   STRAUS, OSCAR. "Roger Williams" in The Origin of the Republican Form of Government in the United States of America. New York: G. P. Putnam's Sons. Chapter 3.
    Focuses on Williams as the earliest champion of soul liberty in America. Contains biography of Williams and a study of his contributions to the republican form of government that were more significant and earlier than Lord Baltimore in Maryland.

1927 A BOOKS

1   BONDY, JOSEPH. How Religious Liberty Was Written into The American Constitution: A History. Syracuse: n.p.
    This pamphlet attributes religious freedom in America and in the Constitution solely to Williams's efforts. Offers little factual support for assertions.

1927 B SHORTER WRITINGS

1   BELMONT, PERRY. Political Equality from Roger Williams to Jefferson. New York: Knickerbocker Press, pp. 107-132.
    Sees Williams as one of small group of men who contributed greatly to the concept of religious freedom in the world. Presents history of religious toleration and shows Williams's place within this area. Williams's principles important not only to Rhode Island but also to the United States. Cites Bancroft (1843.B1) as important analysis of Williams's fame.

2   FREUND, MICHAEL. "Roger Williams," in Der Idee Toleranz Im England Der Grossen Revolution. Halle: Max Niemeyer, pp. 241-268.
    Argues that Williams saw the civil power of the state as developing from the natural order and having no relation to the spiritual world. Sees Williams's stand on religious liberty as logical development of his ideas on separation of powers. Explains relationship of Williams to pamphlet literature in English Civil War.

3   PARRINGTON, VERNON LOUIS. "Roger Williams, Seeker" in Main Currents in American Thought. New York: Harcourt Brace. I: 62-75.
    In chapter entitled "Roger Williams, Seeker," presents thesis that Williams was an early democrat and that his ideas about church-state relationships were derivative from his fundamental concept of the state. Sees the central problem in earlier writers understanding Williams as

1927

>   (PARRINGTON, VERNON LOUIS)
>   a failure to realize the basic relationship of Williams's ideas to the democratic ideas of Jefferson and Franklin. "No other man in New England comprehended so fully the difficulties involved in the problem, as Roger Williams, or examined them so thoroughly; and out of his long speculations emerged a theory of the commonwealth that must be reckoned the richest contribution of Puritanism to American political thought." Shows how Williams attempted to set up the necessary machinery of government in Providence. Ultimately sees Williams's debate with Cotton as a difference between two schools of political theory.

1928 A BOOKS

1   CHAPIN, HOWARD MILLAR. Roger Williams and the King's Colors. Providence: Society of Colonial Wars, E. L. Freeman.
    Presents the documentary evidence dealing with the incident in 1634 when the English flag was defaced by having the cross removed from it. Describes the records of the event by Hubbard (1680.B1) and Winthrop (1649.B2) and explains how this incident involved Williams, as the minister who preached to Endicott. Williams's "flag" with the red cross removed became an official ensign of various foot soldiers from several towns from 1635 on.

2   ERNST, JAMES E. "The Political Thought of Roger Williams." Ph.D. dissertation, University of Washington.
    Argues that Williams's ideas on religious toleration and the relationship between church and state are derived from his fundamental political philosophy. Examines Williams's political philosophy as it is presented in The Bloudy Tenent. Compares Williams's ideas involving the church and state in relation to medieval and renaissance views. "In his political thought, as in his religious, he remained until the end of life a Searcher and Seeker after ultimate truth." See (1929.A1).

3   HALEY, J. W. Roger Williams and Other Famous Rhode Islanders. Providence, n.p.
    Guidebook pamphlet of local history. Includes early history of Providence and Williams's role in it.

1928 B SHORTER WRITINGS

1   ANON. "The Evaluation of Roger Williams' Work," Rhode Island Historical Society Collections, 21 (Jan.), 16.

Brief notice praising Parrington's Main Currents and the treatment of Williams. "Every Rhode Islander if not every American should give thanks for this sympathetic and comprehensive account of the founder of our state."

2   CHAPIN, HOWARD MILLAR. "Roger Williams and the King's Colors," Rhode Island Historical Society Collections, 21: 63.
Brief note on 1928.A1.

1929 A BOOKS

1   ERNST, JAMES E. The Political Thought of Roger Williams. Seattle: University of Washington Press.
The basic origin of Williams's ideas of religious toleration are his ideas of the state. "In his theory of state and the practice of it, Williams belonged to no particular group of political thinkers. In his political thought, as in his religious, he remained until the end of life a Searcher and Seeker after ultimate truth." Examines various theories of state and shows how these influenced Williams's practice and writings.

1929 B SHORTER WRITINGS

1   ANON. "Roger Williams Ancestry," Rhode Island Historical Society Collections, 22 (Jan.), 15-16.
Indicates that a clue to tracing James Williams's ancestry [Williams's father] may be found in recent article by Waters (1893.B2) that refers to a Williams of St. Albans married in 1584 and who died in 1619. Possible relationship to Williams.

2   ERNST, JAMES E. "New Light on Roger Williams' Life in England," Rhode Island Historical Society Collections, 22 (Oct.), 97-103.
Discusses the letters of Sir William and Lady Masham regarding Williams's early life in England. Information is found in two letters written by Williams to Lady Barrington about 1629-30.

1930 A BOOKS

1   EASTON, EMILY. Roger Williams: Prophet and Pioneer. Boston: Houghton Mifflin.
Biography of Williams with particular emphasis on his life in England and conditions of seventeenth-century London. Devotes great deal of attention to Williams's

1930

    (EASTON, EMILY)
writings, especially the controversial works. Also includes passages from the correspondence with Mrs. Sadleir and early colonial records of Providence involving Williams. Offers extensive quotations from Williams's writings as well as contemporaries.

2   GALLUP, CLARENCE M. <u>Return of Roger Williams</u>. Providence.
Examines need for a return to the principles of Williams and his concern for the rights of his fellow man. Copy in Brown University Library, Providence.

1930 B SHORTER WRITINGS

1   HAM, MASON. "Roger Williams," <u>Boston Herald</u> (5 May), p. 13.
Brief notice of importance of Williams's ideas and biography of him.

2   PEARSON, MILO E. "Roger Williams," <u>Essex Institute Historical Collections</u>, 66: 291-316.
Biographical study of Williams's life from birth to period just prior to banishment from Boston. Focuses on the incidents in both Plymouth and Salem related to Williams's life. Concludes with brief introduction to Williams in Providence, charter, etc.

3   SCHNEIDER, HERBERT W. <u>The Puritan Mind</u>. New York: Henry Holt and Company, Reprinted, Ann Arbor: University of Michigan Press, 1958, pp. 53-66.
Presents Williams and Hutchinson as two outstanding examples of the battles for religious toleration. Discusses the treatment of Williams in Mather (1702.B1) and Williams's own defence in <u>The Bloody Tenent</u>, against John Cotton.

1931 A BOOKS - NONE

1931 B SHORTER WRITINGS

1   BRASCH, FREDERICK E. "References to the Royal Society of London and Its Influences upon Scientific Thought in the American Colonies," <u>Scientific American</u>, 127: 9.
Cites facts that Williams was named a member of the Society by his election in 1663. <u>See</u> (1932.B2).

2   ERNST, JAMES E. "Roger Williams and the English Revolution," <u>Rhode Island Historical Society Collections</u>, 24, no. 1

(Jan.), 1-58, 118-128.
Explains Williams's role in the revolution and offers various examples of attacks that were written against The Bloudy Tenent.

3   IVES, J. MOSS. "Roger Williams, Apostle of Religious Bigotry," Thought, 6: 478-492.
A study of the similarities in ideas of intolerance of Williams and other Puritans of his day. Asserts that "When he [Williams] came he was as narrow and bigoted as were any of the Puritans of his day." Ives argues that Lord Baltimore and the Pilgrims of St. Mary in Maryland have a more rightful claim to being apostles of religious liberty than Williams.

4   PARKES, HENRY BAMFORD. "John Cotton and Roger Williams Debate Toleration, 1644-1652," New England Quarterly, 4 (Oct.), 735-756.
Sees Williams as a rational philosopher who could find no peace within the confines of a church because of his tremendous intellectual energy. In the debate with Cotton Williams represented the secularist position which could not accept the Puritan church because it left no room for toleration. Williams's position represented the progressive element in Puritanism that later led to free thought, toleration and democracy in America.

1932 A BOOKS

1   ERNST, JAMES E. Roger Williams: New England Firebrand. New York: The Macmillan Company.
Biography of Williams expanding on the thoughts of earlier book by Ernst (1929.A1). Sees Williams's philosophy as basically democratic and thus the foundation of his ideas on religious toleration. Offers new insights on Williams's life in England.

1932 B SHORTER WRITINGS

1   DAVIS, DAVID. "The First Republican Form of Government in America," Ohio Archeological and Historical Quarterly, 41: 108-114.
Presents arguments about Rhode Island being the first example of republican government over claims of John Wheelwright at Exeter, New Hampshire. Williams's role was critical in setting up the colony at Providence.

Roger Williams: A Reference Guide

1932

2   TILLEY, WINTHROP. "Roger Williams of Providence, not F. R. S.," Rhode Island Historical Society Collections, 25 (July), 87-89.
    Denies that Williams was a member or fellow of the Royal Society of London. Examines evidence of Brasch (see 1931.B1) and concludes that the Roger Williams named to society must be a different person with same name.

1933 A BOOKS - NONE

1933 B SHORTER WRITINGS

1   FREUND, MICHAEL. "Roger Williams, Apostle of Complete Religious Liberty." Translated by James Ernst. Rhode Island Historical Society Collections, 26 (Oct.), 101-133.
    Williams saw the civil power of the state as developing from the natural order and having no relation to the spiritual world. Sees Williams's stand on religious liberty as logical development of his idea on separation of powers. Translated and reprinted from Freund's Der Idee Toleranz Im England Der Grossen Revolution (See 1927.B3).

1934 A BOOKS

1   CHAPIN, HOWARD MILLAR. The Trading Post of Roger Williams. Providence: Society of Colonial Wars, E. L. Freeman Co.
    Discusses trading post of Williams set up at Wickford Point about six miles from Providence. Williams traded many items like kitchen tools and garden items but refused to trade whiskey as some others had done. House at trading post was not built until after Williams had resided in Providence for awhile but before his second trip to England.

1934 B SHORTER WRITINGS

1   ANON. "Roger Williams' Funeral," Rhode Island Historical Society Collections, 27: 54.
    Note on the ledger citation of Benjamin Harris calling attention to the death and funeral of Williams in 1683. Cites fact that Williams was buried behind his home.

2   HALLER, WILLIAM. The Rise of Puritanism. New York: Columbia University Press.
    Brief discussion of Williams's role as a controversialist in England and the place of Bloudy Tenent in debates.

1935

3 MECKLIN, JOHN M. "A Forthright Dissenter," in The Story of American Dissent. New York: Harcourt Brace, pp. 82-115.
   Study is a corrective to the position of James Ernst (1929.A1). Mecklin discusses the religious position of Williams clearly but does not discuss the aspects of Puritanism that led to Williams's dissent with Bay magistrates. Discusses role of Williams and his attitude toward Quakers.

4 MOEHLMAN, CONRAD HENRY. "The Baptists and Roger Williams," Colgate-Rochester Divinity School Bulletin (Nov.), 23-59.
   Examination of the legends versus the facts in relation to whether or not Williams was ever a Baptist and for how long. Cites facts from Williams's own writings and includes letters and other documents related to Williams's ideas about the Baptist movement in Rhode Island. Concludes that the immediate connection between Williams and Baptists is exceedingly tenuous. Williams was a biblicist and a thorough Calvinist.

5 STEAD, GEORGE ALBERT. "Roger Williams and the Massachusetts Bay," New England Quarterly, 8 (June), 235-257.
   Argues that Williams's banishment was necessary and justified because he was attacking the basic power of the Bay court system to rule over its subjects.

1935 A BOOKS

1 GALLUP, CLARENCE M. Roger Williams Passes By. Northern Baptist Convention, Philadelphia: Judson Press.
   A pageant written for the celebration of the Northern Baptist Convention of the three hundredth anniversary of the establishment by Williams of conscious freedom in matters of religious concernment. Contains text of parts for actors to represent Williams during key conflicts in his life.

1935 B SHORTER WRITINGS

1 ANON. "The Date of Roger Williams' Birth," Rhode Island Historical Society Collections, 28: 112-115.
   Based on the references in his writings Williams was born about 1605-1606. Locates six different references to Williams's age at various points in his life and reconstructs date from these sources.

1935

2 ERNST, JAMES E. "The Roger Williams' Seals in the Egerton Manuscripts," *Rhode Island Historical Society Collections* 28: 65-66.
   Discusses seals of letters by Williams found in Egerton Manuscript in the British Museum. Indicates two different types: fleur-de-lis and rose shaped seal.

3 HARKNESS, REUBEN E. E. "Roger Williams, Prophet of Tomorrow," *Journal of Religion*, 15 (Oct.), 400-425.
   Sees Williams as a prophet in the truest sense because of his love of the people. Also develops the analogy of Williams as a prophet not being understood in his world and more a prophet for our own days. Some discussion of writings.

4 LEWIS, MYRTLE M. "Williams and Allied Lines," *Americana*, 29 (July), 430-450.
   Survey of the Williams family name and only brief treatment of the ancestors and descendents of Williams.

5 MILLER, PERRY G. E. "The Contributions of the Protestant Churches to Religious Liberty in Colonial America," *Church History*, 4: 57-66.
   Contributions of Protestant churches was very slight but Williams was the exception to this. Williams was not popular in his own time and his ideas of religious liberty have been overemphasized in the later evaluations of him. Williams did contribute some ideas of liberal thought.

6 WEINER, FREDERICK B. "Roger Williams' Contribution to Modern Thought," *Rhode Island Historical Society Collections*, 28 (Jan.), 1-20.
   Main focus of Williams's thinking is the idea that the state exists for the people and not the people for the state. Agrees with conclusions of Ernst but sees people of the 1930s as not accepting or ready to accept Williams's ideas. Felt the United States would be better able to cope with the needs of the individual if Williams's ideas concerning the relation between the state and the individual were followed.

1936 A BOOKS

1 CHAPIN, HOWARD MILLAR, ed. *A Key Into the Language of America*. Providence: The Rhode Island and Providence Plantations Tercentenary Committee.
   Contains a brief introduction on the origin of *A Key* and background of Williams's life. Reprinted 1971.B2.

Roger Williams: A Reference Guide

1936

2   GARDINER, GEORGE W. <u>Roger Williams, Peacemaker. An Address delivered at the North Kingston Celebration of the 300th Anniversary of the founding of Rhode Island</u>, Kingston: n.p.
    Pamphlet focuses on the role of Williams as a peacemaker with the Indians in the North Kingston area.

3   STRAUS, ROGER WILLIAMS. <u>Religious Liberty, Civilization's Barometer</u>. Washington, D. C.: National Baptist Memorial Church.
    This speech, delivered at the Roger Williams Tercentenary, National Baptist Memorial Church in Washington, October 18, 1935, asserts that whenever civilization has advanced, religious liberty has accompanied it. Williams was responsible for giving this concept to the world and our civilization in America is better for it.

<u>1936 B SHORTER WRITINGS</u>

1   ANDREWS, CHARLES M. "Roger Williams and the Founding of Rhode Island," in <u>The Colonial Period of American History</u>. 2 vols. New Haven: Yale University Press, I: 7-36.
    Discusses role Williams played in founding Providence and offers a capsule study of his leadership abilities. Sees Williams's major problem as applying practically the concept of freedom, "...he [Williams] knew little about practical government or the business of setting up a strong central organization. He never realized his ideals for the traditions, habits, and limitations of his time were against him...he was constantly thwarted by those elements in the colony which were antagonistic to authority...."

2   ANON. "Illustrations Connected With Roger Williams' Life," <u>Rhode Island Historical Society Collections</u>, 29 (Apr.), 33-44.
    Contains photographs of Williams's sundial and compass as well as places in England associated with Williams's life: Pembroke College, etc. Also includes photos of the apple tree root from grave.

3   ATKINS, W. CLYDE. "Roger Williams, the Pioneer of Religious Liberty," <u>Review and Expositor</u>, 33: 279-91.
    Study of the life and teachings of Williams on the celebration of the three hundredth anniversary (October 18, 1935) of his banishment from Massachusetts. Contains biography and study of his principles of religious liberty.

4   B'NAI B'RITH. <u>Roger Williams Celebration</u>. Philadelphia, n.p., October 25.
    Speeches celebrating religious liberty in America and

1936

(B'NAI B'RITH)
Roger Williams's contributions. Addresses by Cornelius O'Brien, Alfred M. Cohen, and Everett Clinchy, representing Catholic, Jewish and Protestant churches of America. Copy in Rhode Island Historical Society Library, Providence.

5   CHANCELLOR, FRANK B. and HENRY S. EALES. "Roger Williams" in Celebrated Carthusians. London: Phillips Allan. Chapter 1.
Focus is on famous graduates of Charter House School. Asserts that "Roger Williams has inspired doctrines that have moulded the character of American society and whose place in the history of democratic thought has yet to be finally determined." Strongly influenced by Ernst biography (1932.A1).

6   EASTON, EMILY. "Mary Barnard," Rhode Island Historical Society Collections, 29 (July), 65-80.
This article gives new information about Williams's wife and her family background. Presents information in a letter of Lady Masham telling of Williams's upcoming marriage.

7   GROSE, HOWARD B. "Roger Williams," Christian Century, 53 (Feb. 12), 259-262.
Contains biography and study of Williams's ideas of toleration with special attention to his treatment of Jews.

8   HARKNESS, REUBEN E. E. "Principles Established in Rhode Island," Church History, 5 (Sept.), 216-226.
In addition to his importance for the cause of religious liberty, Williams was also responsible for (1) free rights in religion, (2) separation of church and state, (3) representative government, (4) and public ownership of land and natural resources.

9   MASSACHUSETTS HOUSE BILL 488. "Providing For the Revocation of the Sentence of Expulsion Passed on Roger Williams in 1635," Boston: State House Printing Office.
This bill was introduced on the three hundredth anniversary of Williams's expulsion and lifted the banishment decree.

*10 SHAAF, DAVID S. "Was Roger Williams a Nuisance?" The Christian Century (4 March), p. 371.
Cited in Rhode Island Historical Society Library. Not seen.

1938

11 WROTH, LAWRENCE. "Variations in Five Copies of Roger Williams' Key Into the Language of America," Rhode Island Historical Society Collections, 29 (Oct.), 120-121.
    Deals with the textual problems encountered in the various editions of A Key consulted for Chapin's 1936 edition (See 1936.A1).

1937 A BOOKS

1 BROCKUNIER, SAMUEL HUGH. "Roger Williams: A Study of His Life and Career to 1657." Ph.D. dissertation, Harvard University.
    Sees Williams as more of a political thinker involved in the social change in the seventeenth century. Examines Williams's writings and ideas as illustrative of this thesis. Develops the importance of the English political and religious controversies as critical to understanding Williams's position on religious liberty as an outgrowth of his political philosophy.

2 WROTH, LAWRENCE. Roger Williams. Marshall Woods Lecture. Brown University Papers, 14. Providence: Brown University Press.
    Concentrates on Williams's missionary role to the Indians. Places Williams's work with Indians in proper perspective. Sees Williams's primary concern in saving the Indians rather than freedom of conscience.

1937 B SHORTER WRITINGS - NONE

1938 A BOOKS - NONE

1938 B SHORTER WRITINGS

1 JORDAN, WILBUR K. The Development of Religious Toleration in England. 4 vols. Cambridge: Harvard University Press. III: 475-477.
    Discussion of Williams in connection with toleration movement in England. Sees Williams's position on religious persecution as leading to his liberalized stand on freedom of theology.

2 PIERCY, JOSEPHINE K. Studies in Literary Types in Seventeenth Century America. Yale Studies in English No. 91. New Haven: Yale University Press.
    Refers to Williams's A Key as an example of the blend of scientific and literary works in seventeenth century.

1938

    3   RUSTERHOLTZ, WALLACE P. "Roger Williams: The First American" in <u>American Heretics and Saints</u>. Boston: Manthorne & Burack. Chapter 2.
        Focuses on Williams as the first American because of his concept of freedom of religion.

1939 A BOOKS

    1   DENISON, MERRILL. <u>Haven of the Spirit</u>. New York: Dramatists' Play Service.
        A play about Williams in which he is cast as the central character. Focuses on his settling of Providence and stand on religious liberty.

    2   LONGACRE, CHARLES SMULL. <u>Roger Williams: His Life, Work, and Ideals</u>. Washington, D. C.: Review and Herald Publishing Company.
        Biography of Williams that calls forth the ideals in his life to awaken Americans in the beginning of World War II. Sees Williams as a hero needed in our modern age and examines his deeds from this perspective.

1939 B SHORTER WRITINGS

    1   BROCKUNIER, SAMUEL F. "Roger Williams and the Democratic Faith," in <u>Exercises at Dedication of Roger Williams Monument</u>. Providence: Roger Williams Memorial Association.
        Discusses the conception of democracy in Williams's writings and quotes from his work. We can see a clear insight into democracy by examining Williams's ideas today.

    2   SEAGER, ALLAN. <u>They Worked For A Better World</u>. New York: Macmillan, pp. 12-33.
        Devotes one chapter to Williams and explains his contribution as "the first man to take the idea of a civil democratic state, with complete freedom of religion, and make it work."

1940 A BOOKS

    1   BACH, MARCUS. <u>Roger Williams: A Play of Democracy</u>. Boston: Walter Baker Company.
        A play about Williams and his heroic deeds designed primarily for secondary school audiences.

2   BROCKUNIER, SAMUEL HUGH. The Irrepressible Democrat: Roger Williams. New York: Ronald Press.
    Main thesis is that Williams represented the beginnings of social revolt in America and that "more than any other in the English colonies epitomized the revolutionary forces of his age. I have intended not to eulogize him as unique in his century but to demonstrate his relevance to his own times." Study is both biography and study of how Williams was misunderstood in his own times because he represented the wave of the future. Detailed analysis of both the social and political conditions of Williams's life in London, Salem, and Boston. Finally, Williams was a person who represented the upthrust of democratic ideals and would not be suppressed. Review in New England Quarterly for December 1940 and Rhode Island Historical Society Collections, 24 (1941), 57-59.

3   POTEAT, EDWIN McNEIL. Roger Williams Redivivus, being an address delivered at the Northern Baptist Convention, Atlantic City, May, 1940. New York: Northern Baptist Convention, The Ministers and Missionaries Benefit Board.
    Speech deals with Williams as a Baptist and the first advocate of religious liberty. Calls attention to need for adherence to his idea of faith and concern for his fellow man.

1940 B SHORTER WRITINGS - NONE

1941 A BOOKS - NONE

1941 B SHORTER WRITINGS

1   DOS PASSOS, JOHN. "Roger Williams and the Planting of the Commonwealth in America," in The Ground We Stand On. New York: Harcourt Brace, pp. 21-158.
    Biography of Williams emphasizes his contributions to America. Dos Passos's manner of writing offers a new approach to telling Williams's story. Attributes to Williams the task of bringing "the seeds of a whole civilization" to a new country.

2   HIRSCH, ELIZABETH FEIST. "John Cotton and Roger Williams: Their Controversy Concerning Religious Liberty," Church History, 10 (March), 38-51.
    Analyzes the intellectual background and the various arguments put forth by both participants. "Cotton confronted his conception of a visible church with Williams'

1941

(HIRSCH, ELIZABETH FEIST)
conception of an invisible. It seems strange that they were not aware of this discrepancy. It made any attempt to come to an understanding between them hopeless." Concludes that Cotton was much more of a Calvinist than Williams but not necessarily a more typical Puritan.

1942 A BOOKS - NONE

1942 B SHORTER WRITINGS

1   BARKER, ARTHUR. Milton and the Puritan Dilemma. Toronto: University of Toronto Press.
    Brief discussion of Williams in England and the toleration controversy in the various tracts.

2   NEWMAN, LOUIS ISRAEL. "Roger Williams, The Bible, and Religious Liberty," Opinion, 12 , no. 5 (March), 6-7.
    Calls for attention to Williams's ideals in these trying times for religious liberty. Focuses on Williams's use of Bible in the wording of his laws on religious liberty and toleration.

3   SAVELLE, MAX. "Roger Williams," in Foundations of American Civilization: A History of Colonial America. New York: Henry Holt, pp. 148-157.
    Sees Williams as alone as a liberal democrat against the Puritan establishment.

4   SWAN, BRADFORD F. "A Plymouth Friend of Roger Williams," Rhode Island History, 1: 94-95.
    Describes Williams's friendship with Dr. Samuel Fuller and the bequest left by Fuller to Williams in his will.

5   SWEET, WILLIAM WARREN. Religion in Colonial America. New York: Charles Scribner's Sons, pp. 122-130.
    Provides study of Williams in relation to the development of religion in America and particularly the development of other religious colonies like Rhode Island. Presents examination of Williams's work like Bloudy Tenent as well as a brief survey of scholarship on Williams up to Brockunier's biography. Analysis of Williams's concept of religious liberty in his writings.

Roger Williams: A Reference Guide

1944 A BOOKS

1   EATON, JEANETTE. Lone Journey: The Life of Roger Williams. New York: Harcourt Brace.
    Fictional narration of Williams's life designed for children.

2   SWAN, BRADFORD F. The Case of Richard Chasmore, alias Long Dick. Providence: Roger Williams Press.
    One of the many incidents where Williams acted as judge in early Providence. Chasmore was accused of sodomy and ordered to appear before Williams in Providence on charges of bestiality.

1944 B SHORTER WRITINGS

1   HARRIS, HUGH. "Roger Williams Visits London, 1644," British Weekly, 29 June, p. 1.
    Williams's visit to London is recalled by Harris as a means to rally the public to the courage and dedication needed to face the threats of war. He also speculates on what Williams would have thought about Christian countries like England going to war with Germany.

2   SWAN, BRADFORD F. "An Unpublished Letter of Roger Williams," Rhode Island History, 3 (Oct.), 139-140.
    Brief note on and text of a letter written by Williams to the Town of Providence between 27 October 1660 and 14 March 1661/62. Letter was given to society and had not been previously published.

1945 A BOOKS - NONE

1945 B SHORTER WRITINGS

1   MORELAND, MARC. "Roger Williams: Discipline for Today," Phylon, 6 (2nd Quarter), 136-140.
    Suggests the importance of "such first principles as were conceived and projected by Roger Williams, the great democratic theoretician and experimenter of the seventeenth century." Sees most valuable attribute of Williams as his political attitudes.

2   WILLISON, GEORGE F. Saints and Strangers. New York: Reynal and Hitchcock. Reprinted, Time-Life Books, 1964, pp. 373-378.
    Presents biography of Williams and his dealings with

1945

(WILLISON, GEORGE F.)
Cotton, Winthrop and the colony at Plymouth. Compares his treatment to Hutchinson and other dissenters.

1946 A BOOKS - NONE

1946 B SHORTER WRITINGS

1 PEATTIE, DONALD. "Roger Williams, First Modern American," Reader's Digest, 49 (Dec.), 65-69.
   Biography and study of Williams's contributions to democracy in America. Williams's ideas of democracy and his concept of liberty with law and order was the same as ours at its best.

2 SWAN, BRADFORD F. "Roger Williams and the Insane," Rhode Island History, 5: 65-70.
   Uses several letters by Williams to show that he felt it was the duty of the civil government to care for the insane and look out for their welfare. Includes two individual cases, Mrs. Adam Goodwin and Mrs. Robert Pike, where Williams interceded on behalf of the insane and helped them.

1948 A BOOKS

1 RODDY, CLARENCE S. "The Religious Thought of Roger Williams." Ph.D. dissertation, New York University.
   Discusses the Calvinistic background of Williams's religious beliefs and the importance of understanding them in relation to his controversial works. Point of departure for Roddy is a fundamental disagreement with the conclusions of Ernst (See 1929.A1) on the basis of Williams's political thought. Examines the various tenets of Calvinism and illustrates them in Williams's writings.

1948 B SHORTER WRITINGS

1 RODDY, CLARENCE S. "The Religious Thought of Roger Williams," Abstracts of Theses, New York: New York University, pp. 125-132.
   Discusses the Calvinistic background of Williams's theology and the basic ideas in his controversial works. Point of departure for Roddy is a fundamental disagreement with James Ernst (1929.A1) on Williams. See 1941.A1.

1949 A BOOKS

1   ANTHONY, BERTHA WILLIAMS and C. H. WOOD WEEDEN. Roger Williams of Providence. Cranston, R. I.: n.p.
    This is a comprehensive listing of Williams's descendents from the seventeenth to the twentieth century. It includes all related to Williams in a direct line. Current to 1948.

1949 B SHORTER WRITINGS

1   PEATTIE, DONALD. "Roger Williams, Seeker" in American Heartwood. New York: Houghton Mifflin, pp. 87-106.
    Elaborates on Williams's struggle against the magistrates and his long struggle in the wilderness in winter.

2   SWAN, BRADFORD F. Gregory Dexter of London and New England, 1610-1700. Rochester, New York: Printing House of L. Hart.
    This book is a biography of Williams's printer for A Key and details information about the relationship between the two. Includes texts of letters exchanged between them.

3   _____. "Roger Williams' Manuscripts in the Rhode Island Historical Society Library," Rhode Island History, 6: 91-94.
    Contains list of manuscripts owned by society written by Williams. Updates Chapin (1918.A3) by adding some new items. Cites Massachusetts Historical Society and Providence City Hall as locations of other Williams's materials.

1950 A BOOKS

1   REES, GILBERT. I Seek a City. New York: Dutton.
    Story of Williams written for children in fictional form.

1950 B SHORTER WRITINGS

1   MOORE, JOHN A. "Roger Williams," Baptist Quarterly Incorporated, 13: 244-52.
    Presents biography of Williams focusing on his life in England and his decision to go to New England. Discussion of his principles of liberty and his leadership of Providence colony. Sees Williams as leader whose ideas on democracy were not original with him but nonetheless were given their fullest expression by him and have been followed.

1951

1951 A BOOKS

1   HUDSON, WINTHROP, ed. "Introduction" in *Experiments of Spiritual Life and Health*. Philadelphia: The Westminster Press, pp. 1-11.
    Introduction demonstrates the strong theological basis of Williams's lesser known controversial tracts. Calls attention to the concept in Williams's *Experiments* of serving God for his sake alone, as well as Williams's concern for freeing ourselves from worldly considerations. Disputes the interpretations of Ernst (1929.A1) and Parrington (1927.B3).

1951 B SHORTER WRITINGS

1   BAINTON, ROLAND H. "The Seeker," in *The Travail of Religious Liberty: Nine Biographical Sketches*. Philadelphia: The Westminster Press, pp. 208-228.
    Discussion of Williams and his relation to Calvinism. Stresses the tolerant spirit of Williams as one of his best assets.

2   HUDSON, WINTHROP. "Roger Williams, No Secularist," *Christian Century*, 68 (22 Aug.), 963-964.
    Hudson takes exception to Parrington's (1927.B3) estimation of Williams. Shows how Williams's *Experiments of Spiritual Life and Health* deals with three aspects: (1) shortness of time in life, (2) the importance of freeing ourselves of the world, (3) the necessity of serving God for his sake alone. Emphasizes religious approach to Williams.

3   MORRIS, MAXWELL H. "Roger Williams and the Jews," *American Jewish Archives*, 3, no. 2 (Jan.), 24-27.
    Cites direct statements in Williams's writings about the Jews and shows how Williams thought Christianity superior. Williams was a "political liberal in religious matters but not a religious liberal." Williams's tolerance may not be that tolerant in his conception of all religions not being of equal worth.

4   ROSSITER, CLINTON L. "Roger Williams on the Anvil of Experience," *American Quarterly*, 3 (Jan.), 14-21.
    Describes Williams as "an early exemplar of the American tradition of political pragmatism." Considers Williams the first American political thinker and emphasizes the political climate of early Rhode Island. Sees Williams's theology as dominant but necessary to understanding his

political philosophy too. Concludes that the practical experience of leading Rhode Island taught Williams the importance of arbitration, rights and duties, equality, pluralism, economic determinism, and change. Cites evidence in writings and private letters.

1952 A BOOKS

1   THOMPSON, LUTHER JOE. "A Study of Roger Williams' Thought with Special Reference to his Conception of Religious Liberty." Ph.D. dissertation, University of Edinburgh, Scotland.
    Examines the philosophical question of religious liberty and applies specific ideas about the concept to Williams's writings. Begins with a long detailed study of the history of religious liberty in the world. Presents brief overview of subject in Williams's time, a discussion of religious liberty in Williams's life, and finally the use of it in Williams's writings. Concludes that Williams's importance "does not lie in his contributions to the philosophical foundations of religious liberty," but rather "in the realm of practical application" of the ideas in his writings and in his leadership in Providence.

1952 B SHORTER WRITINGS

1   CALAMANDREI, MAURO. "Neglected Aspects of Roger Williams' Thought," Church History, 21 (Sept.), 239-258.
    Presents the view of Williams as a Puritan of the seventeenth century. Main divisions focus on (1) Williams's seekerism, skepticism, and individualism are confined to problems of church and ministry, (2) Williams's doctrines of church, his belief in principles, and the visible church are related to a prophetic reading of history, (3) for Williams the role of the magistrate in the commonwealth is not only to restrain evil and administer order but primarily to secure freedom for the Spirit and Word of God, Concludes with discussion of connections between Williams's theology and political theory.

2   HOLMAN, WINNIFRED L. "Roger Williams," American Genealogist, 28 (Oct.), 197-209.
    An analysis of Williams's family records and origins in both England and Wales. Primarily concerned with immediate ancestors of Williams.

3   MORISON, SAMUEL ELIOT, ed. Of Plymouth Plantation, 1620-1647 by William Bradford. New York: Alfred A. Knopf.
    Contains Index to Bradford's discussions of Williams. (See 1647.B1.)

Roger Williams: A Reference Guide

1953

1953 A BOOKS

1   CALAMANDREI, MAURO. "The Theology and Political Thought of Roger Williams." Ph.D. dissertation, University of Chicago.
    Demonstrates that "rather than being a man of the Renaissance and the Enlightenment Roger Williams was a Puritan." Examines the various works of Williams to show how his noncontroversial works are important to an understanding of his theology. Shows how his theology and political philosophy are related.

2   MILLER, PERRY. Roger Williams. His Contribution to the American Tradition. New York: Bobbs-Merrill.
    Selections from Williams's writings and discussion of them. Contends that Williams was not more modern than his contemporary Puritans but that he was precisely more Puritan than they were. Demonstrates (1) the importance of Williams's reliance upon typology, (2) the small effect if any that Williams had on the founding fathers or the concept of democracy in America, (3) the basic position of Williams as a controversialist, theologian, and political leader rather than as an heroic liberal-democrat. Reviewed in New York Times for September 27, 1953 and Providence Journal, January 24, 1955.

1953 B SHORTER WRITINGS

1   HUDSON, WINTHROP. "Faith and Freedom" in The Great Tradition of American Churches. New York: Harper and Row. Chapters 1-3, 11.
    Discusses the concept of church and state in Williams's ideas. Relates Williams's ideas to the subsequent development of churches in America.

2   ROSSITER, CLINTON L. "Roger Williams" in Seedtime of the Republic. New York: Harcourt Brace, pp. 179-204.
    Shows how the practical experience of leading Providence taught Williams many things about democracy in practice. (See 1951.B4.)

1955 A BOOKS - NONE

1955 B SHORTER WRITINGS

1   ADELMAN, DAVID C. "Roger Williams and the Jews," Rhode Island Jewish Historical Association, 1, iii (June), 149-157.
    Cites relevant passages in Williams's works dealing with

the Jews. Points out that "it was Williams who interceded for the readmission of Jews into England and never lost an opportunity while in England to plead their cause."

2   CLEAL, CLIFFORD H. "Roger Williams," in <u>Baptists Who Made History</u>. Edited by A. S. Clement. London: Carey Kingsgate Press, pp. 19-27.

    General discussion of Williams as Baptist who developed religious liberty in Rhode Island. Focuses on the religious aspects of Williams's writings and his work with the Indians.

3   DAWSON, JOSEPH. "Roger Williams and the Pattern of the American Republic," <u>Quarterly Baptist Review</u>, 15, no. 2, 9-16.

    Argues that the ideas of Thomas Jefferson presented in the <u>Declaration of Independence</u> and the <u>Virginia Statutes on Religious Freedom</u> are traceable to ideas contained in Williams's thought and writings. Bases argument on three assumptions: (1) the similarity of ideas in the <u>Declaration</u> and Williams's writings, (2) the presence of Winthrop's <u>Journal</u> in Jefferson's library at Monticello, (3) direct contact between Jefferson and Baptist teachers and ministers on the subject of religious liberty.

4   HALLER, WILLIAM. <u>Liberty and Reformation in the Puritan Revolution</u>. New York: Columbia University Press, pp. 151-159.

    Chapter entitled "Church and State in New England: John Cotton and Roger Williams," examines the basis of the debate between Williams and John Cotton.

1956 A BOOKS - NONE

1956 B SHORTER WRITINGS

1   BURLINGAME, ROGER. "Zion in the Forest," <u>American Heritage Magazine</u>, 7 (June), 34-37.

    Brief survey of Williams's life. Distinguishes between realistic and romantic viewpoints among biographies written about him.

2   CARMER, CARL, ed. <u>Cavalcade of America</u>. New York: Crown Publishers, pp. 145-148.

    Brief treatment of Williams told in fictional form. Primarily concerned with biography.

1956

3   DAWSON, JOSEPH MARTIN. "Roger Williams and the Pattern of the American Republic," in Baptists and the American Republic. Nashville: Broadman Press, pp. 15-45.
    Discusses the relationship between Williams's ideas on religious freedom and the ideas of Thomas Jefferson in Declaration of Independence. Suggests reasons for comparison. See 1955.B3.

4   NIEBUHR, RICHARD. The Kingdom of God in America. Hamden: Shoestring Press, p. 68.
    Contends that Williams was a theologian much more than he was a political scientist. Takes issue with those like Ernst (1929.A1) who see his contribution as primarily politically oriented.

5   SIMPSON, ALAN. "How Democratic Was Roger Williams?" William and Mary Quarterly, 3rd ser., 13 (Feb.), 53-67.
    Argues that Parrington (1927.B3), Ernst (1929.A1), and Brockunier (1940.A2) are wrong in asserting the democratic principle in Williams's thought and that the reason for this is a misreading of the essential importance of Christian ideas of love and freedom of worship in Williams's ideas. "There is no trace whatever in Roger Williams of that gradual secularization of interest which is a marked feature in the history of the Levellers...There is every evidence that his principle of religious liberty was derived both formally and emotionally from his sense of what was due to God."

1957 A BOOKS

1   EDWARDS, CECILE PEPIN. Roger Williams, Defender of Freedom. New York: Grove Press.
    Story of Williams's life written for children.

2   JOHNSON, ALBERT. Roger Williams and Mary. New York: Friendship Press.
    Play written about Williams and his wife and designed for a juvenile audience.

3   SCHEVILL, JAMES. The Bloody Tenent: A Play. Belfast, Maine: Porter.
    Play dealing with trial of Roger Williams that led to his banishment. Copy in Providence Public Library, Providence, Rhode Island.

4 WHITE, ELIZABETH NICHOLSON. Mary Barnard, Wife of Roger Williams. Providence: Watchemoket Press.
   A pamphlet that assembles all of the information known about Mary Barnard and includes references to Williams's writings in letters to her.

5 WINSLOW, OLA ELIZABETH. Master Roger Williams. New York: Macmillan.
   Biography of Williams focusing on the different roles Williams played during his lifetime: pensioner, chaplain, roving ambassador, linguist, trader, controversialist, and colony agent. Detailed examination of the London of Williams's day and the more important incidents that happened during his years in England. Stresses the important work Williams did with the Indians and their friendship for him. Offers broad panorama of the various locations associated with Williams's life such as Boston, Salem, London, and Providence. Also includes a selected bibliography of writings about Williams. Reviewed in New York Times and New York Herald Tribune for October 20, 1957.

1957 B SHORTER WRITINGS

1 WINSLOW, OLA ELIZABETH. "The Religion of Roger Williams, 1632-1672," Congregational Library Bulletin, 8 (May), 5-13.
   Examines changing perspectives of Williams's religious ideas from his early life in New England to his debate with the Quakers in 1672. See 1957.A3. Discusses how Williams has been misunderstood because of confusion between his political and religious beliefs. Experiments of Spiritual Life and Health and George Fox Digg'd out of his Burrowes best sources of Williams's religious beliefs.

2 WOODWARD, CARL R. "Roger Williams and Rhode Island's Contribution to Democracy," Liberty (2 May), 17-20.
   Draws comparison between Thomas Jefferson and Williams on the various aspects of democracy. Presents Williams as a liberal democrat that laid cornerstone of the republic.

1958 A BOOKS - NONE

1958 B SHORTER WRITINGS

1 GAUSTAD, EDWIN S. "Roger Williams and the Principle of Separation," Foundations, 1 (Jan.), 55-64.
   Considers Williams's concept of separation from three points of view: (1) separation of the Massachusetts

1958

(GAUSTAD, EDWIN S.)
churches from the Church of England, (2) separation of ecclesiastical from civil government, (3) separation of Christianity from culture. Considers arguments of Williams with Cotton and the evidence in Williams's writings including The Bloudy Tenent.

2 GUMMERE, RICHARD M. "Church, State, and the Classics: The Cotton-Williams Debate," Classical Journal, 54 (Nov.), 175-183.
Examines the classical tradition and its influence on both participants in the famous debate. Finds Cotton more theological in debate, with Williams employing a wider range of knowledge. Williams generally goes further afield in his use of classical sources. Discusses The Bloudy Tenent, BT Washed, and BT Yet More Bloudy. Williams combined his use of mystical symbolism with a wider sweep of classical illustrations than Cotton. (See 1963.B2.)

3 MUELLER, DAVID L. "Roger Williams on the Church and Ministry," Review and Expositor, 55 (April), 165-181.
Discusses the importance of understanding Williams's thought in relation to the central significance he placed on the concepts of election and justification. Attempts "to show the manner in which the related doctrines of the Church and ministry provide us with a part of the theological framework within which the rather enigmatic life and thought of Roger Williams became intelligible."

1959 A BOOKS - NONE

1959 B SHORTER WRITINGS

1 LOWENHERZ, ROBERT J. "Roger Williams and the Great Quaker Debate," American Quarterly, 11: ii, 157-165.
Sees Williams as the middle position between the emphasis on complete individuality of the Quaker sect on one hand and the complete authority of the state over the individual represented by Massachusetts. Presents the Quaker debates of 1672 as an indication of the liberal treatment Williams allowed toward them in his colony of Rhode Island.

1961 A BOOKS

1 CRICHTON, ROBERT JOCELYN. "Roger Williams on Church and State." Ph.D. dissertation, Teachers College, Columbia University.
   An examination of the motives behind Williams's ideas of the relationship between church and state. Attempts "to show that Roger Williams had a prior concern for New Testament religion and God's rights over His own kingdom. It also reveals that he had little interest in philosophies of government for the nations of this world." Examines legends about Williams and compares these with the facts from his writings about the church and civil government.

2 GANNON, FRED A. <u>Roger Williams, Thinker, Speaker, Founder, and Teacher</u>. Salem, Mass.: J. N. Simard.
   Ten page pamphlet on biography of Williams and selections from his writings. Copy in Rhode Island Historical Society Library.

3 PAYNE, ERNEST ALEXANDER. <u>Roger Williams</u>. London: Independent Press Ltd. 14 pp.
   Brief biography of Williams with special emphasis on his work with the Indians and his contributions toward religious liberty in America. Discusses the major works of Williams in brief and relates them to the seventeenth-century controversies over religious freedom. Contains brief bibliography at end.

1961 B SHORTER WRITINGS

1 BROWNE, BENJAMIN. "Roger Williams--A Pioneer of Liberty" in <u>Tales Of Baptist Daring</u>. Philadelphia: The Judson Press, pp. 11-19.
   Book for young Baptist children to teach them about such famous Baptists as Williams, John Bunyan, and Isaac Backus. Treatment of Williams combines biography with "historical imagination" to retell Williams's story.

1962 A BOOKS - NONE

1962 B SHORTER WRITINGS

1 JANTZ, HAROLD, ed. <u>First Century of New England Verse</u>. New York, pp. 7-8.
   Presents a selection of Williams's poems from <u>A Key</u>. Describes Williams as "the finest poet amongst the heretics."

1962

2   SCHULTZ, HAROLD J. "Roger Williams, Delinquent Saint: The Religious Odyssey of the Providence Prophet," Baptist Quarterly, 19 (April), 253-269.
    Study deals with Williams's beliefs as they are represented in his actions and writings. One key to understanding Williams was his all important concept of the separation of powers between the church and the state.

3   TERRIS, WALTER FRANKLIN. "The Right to Speak in Massachusetts, 1628-1685." Ph.D. dissertation, Northwestern University.
    Examines the role of the magistrates in controlling freedom of speech in Massachusetts and their problems with Hutchinson, Williams, and others.

4   ZIFF, LARZER. The Career of John Cotton: Puritanism and the American Experience. Princeton: Princeton University Press, pp. 212-222.
    Presents careful study of Cotton and Williams debate. Explains, "at a time when he [Cotton] was concerned with maintaining his view of the church body as a community of Professed believers against powerful antagonists who were anxious to broaden the base of church membership, Cotton also became engaged in a battle against one who opposed his polity as being too broad and insufficiently refined and separated from corruption." Also includes a brief chronology of publications in the debate. Reviewed in New England Quarterly, 36 (April), pp. 263-65.

1963 A BOOKS - NONE

1963 B SHORTER WRITINGS

1   CAMP, LEON R. "Roger Williams vs. 'The Upstarts': The Rhode Island Debates of 1672," Quaker History, 52 (Autumn), 69-76.
    Analyzes both the content and context of the debate and offers several distinctions between seventeenth-century ideas of debate and disputation. Evaluates each of the fourteen points developed by Williams. Shows how each day's debate focused on a different issue and how the content and method of Williams's arguments were employed. Concludes, "it is a gross understatement to say that the Rhode Island debates were poor examples of good debating."

2   GUMMERE, RICHARD M. The American Colonial Mind and the Classical Tradition: Essays in Comparative Culture. Cambridge: Harvard University Press, pp. 44-55.

Discusses the use of classical tradition in the debate between Cotton and Williams. (See 1961.B2.)

3   MILLER, PERRY. "Roger Williams: An Essay in Interpretation," in Volume VII, The Complete Writings of Roger Williams. New York: Russell & Russell, pp. 5-25.
    Expansion of earlier ideas on typology from Roger Williams, His Contribution to the American Tradition (1953.A2). Discusses modern studies of Williams and the controversy as related in Winthrop's Journal. Asserts that while Williams was a typologist, Cotton and his colleagues were "federalists." To understand Williams it is necessary to realize that Cotton and Williams differed fundamentally in the way they read and interpreted the Bible. Examines tenets of Calvinism as found in Williams's writings. See 1965.B5.

4   MOORE, LEROY, Jr. "Roger Williams and the Historians," Church History, 32 (Dec.), 432-451.
    Studies the treatment of Williams at the hands of historians from Bradford and Winthrop to the twentieth-century writers like Miller and Brockunier. Survey of the major movements of realistic, romantic, and negative criticism of Williams and his writings.

1964 A BOOKS

1   GREENE, THEODORE P. Roger Williams and the Massachusetts Magistrates. Boston: D. C. Heath.
    Varied reactions to Williams are represented by excerpts from longer works by critics and historians through the centuries since Williams's banishment. Introduction focuses on the relevance of Williams's position on church-state relations for today. Selections include writers from Winthrop and Mather down to the work of Miller and Morgan.

2   NYGAARD, NORMAN E. Champion of Liberty, The Story of Roger Williams. Grand Rapids: Zondervan Publishing House.
    Story of Williams and his deeds told in fictionalized form.

1964 B SHORTER WRITINGS

*1 CAMP, LEON R. "Roger Williams: Rhetoric of Ranting," Today's Speech, 12, no. 3 (Sept.), 21-22.
    Not seen.

Roger Williams: A Reference Guide

1964

2   HUDSON, WINTHROP. "John Locke--Preparing the Way for the Revolution," Journal of Presbyterian History, 42 (March), 19-38.
        Deals with the political ideas of the Puritans including Williams as a strong influence on John Locke and subsequently important to understanding the political background of the American Revolution.

1965 A BOOKS - NONE

1965 B SHORTER WRITINGS

1   BARKER, SHIRLEY. "Roger Williams," in Builders of New England. New York: Dodd Mead, pp. 28-64.
        Devotes one chapter to biography of Williams and his contributions to New England in work with Indians. Discusses the banishment and his discovery of Rhode Island.

2   EMERSON, EVERETT. John Cotton. New York: Twayne Publishers. Chapter 7.
        Offers detailed analysis of Cotton's writings and puts controversy with Williams in proper place. Shows how the controversy with Williams has been blown out of all proportion with the many other events in Cotton's life.

3   MOORE, LEROY, Jr. "Roger Williams as An Enduring Symbol for the Baptists," Journal of Church and State, 7 (Spring), 181-189.
        While the Baptists have not been short on praise for Williams he should be seen in the light of his time period. Williams was not the first Baptist in America nor was he a Baptist for a very long time. John Clarke was more important as first Baptist in America, and John Locke, not Williams, important for religious liberty in the concept of American government.

4   _____. "Religious Liberty, Roger Williams, and the Revolutionary Era," Church History, 34 (March), 57-76.
        Shows how the basic ideas of freedom in American law have developed out of the Lockean philosophy of the eighteenth century and had little if anything to do with Williams. Examines the fundamental Calvinistic basis of Williams's political thought. Concludes by showing that the efforts of Isaac Backus and John Leland supporting the issue of religious liberty and Williams as an archetype of that idea were of secondary importance to the secular movement of Jefferson and Madison.

1966

5   MORGAN, EDMUND. "Miller's Williams," New England Quarterly, 38 (Dec.), 513-523.
    Review of The Complete Writings Of Roger Williams with special emphasis on Miller's "Essay" in Vol. VII (1963.B3). Suggests that the key to Williams is understanding his concept of the relationship between church and state. Feels that Miller overemphasizes the importance of typology. Cites some examples from Williams's texts to support thesis.

6   ROSENMEIER, JESPER. "The Image of Christ: The Typology of John Cotton." Ph.D. dissertation, Harvard University. Chapter 5.
    Demonstrates the importance of typology and Cotton's use of it in the debate with Williams. Main source of the argument for each was the nature of Christ's incarnation and the ways in which both Williams and Cotton employed typology to interpret this. Williams rejected Cotton's belief in the gradual redemption of man. Cites specific examples from the writings of both participants.

7   VAUGHAN, ALDEN T. New England Frontier: Puritans and Indians, 1607-1675. Boston: Little Brown & Co., pp. 119-120, 239-240.
    Study deals with the relations between the Puritans and Indians and has many references to Williams's work with them. Most extensive section is Chapter V dealing with the Pequot War and Williams's role as peacemaker. Index should be consulted for references to Williams, A Key, and his relation with Narragansett Indians.

1966 A BOOKS

1   ANTHONY, BERTHA WILLIAMS. Roger Williams of Providence. Cranston, R.I.: n.p.
    Updates 1949.B1 by including Williams's descendents after 1948. Also includes corrections of earlier genealogy.

2   COVEY, CYCLONE. The Gentle Radical: A Biography of Roger Williams. New York: Macmillan.
    Not a complete biography in itself, but rather, an attempt to bring "a sharper focus on not only Williams himself but the men he interacted with and the power struggle in both England and New England which took place in a moment of intense change--cultural, economic, political, social, and ideological." Focus in various chapters is on Williams in conflict with Cotton, Winthrop, the Pilgrims, and the people of Salem, etc. Examines Williams's life up to 1638 and concludes he was a "gentle radical,"

1966

    (COVEY, CYCLONE)
        able to rise above the occasion to quell differences and maintain peace. Reviewed by Darett Rutman, <u>New England Quarterly</u>, 40 (1967), 282-284.

3   REED, JOHN WILLIAM. "The Rhetoric of A Colonial Controversy: Roger Williams vs. the Massachusetts Bay Colony. Ph.D. dissertation, Ohio State University.
        Demonstrates how Williams's abilities were just as significant in the area of public oration as in public preaching. Analyses the various rhetorical methods employed by both Cotton and Williams. Shows the history of rhetoric in William's time and the type of curriculum at Cambridge University. Cites specific examples from <u>The Bloudy Tenent</u> to illustrate these principles of debate. Concludes that Williams has an important place in the history of public address in America because of his radicalism and his ability in the pamphlet debate with Cotton to defend and counter-attack his accusers.

4   WITHERS, RICHARD E. "Roger Williams and the Rhode Island Colony: A Study in Leadership Roles." Ph.D. Dissertation. Boston University.
        Presents an examination of the various roles that Williams assumed in the founding and early governing of Providence. Begins with a justification and a detailed explanation of Williams's role in leading and governing Rhode Island from a sociological point of view. Categorizes the dominant roles in Williams's life as: (1) ascribed, (2) assumed, (3) symbiotic, (4) crisis. Applies these different role patterns to the various events in Williams's life in Providence. Concludes that Williams was an important force as a religious leader in the early society of Rhode Island and suggests some interesting sidelights about the interpersonal relationships Williams experienced with various dissenting factions both in Providence and surrounding towns. Bases his conclusions on evidence in published writings of Williams as well as private letters.

1966 B SHORTER WRITINGS

1   APTHEKER, HERBERT. "Williams, Hutchinson, and the Witch-Hunt" in <u>The Colonial Era: A History of the American People</u>. New York: International Publishers, pp. 92-109.
        In section on Williams and Hutchinson, describes Williams as attacking both the political and ecclesiastical foundations of the Bay Colony. Disagrees with Miller's estimation of Williams. Concludes that Williams was "one

of the most advanced, consistent, and successful friends of freedom that American history has yet produced."

2   GARRETT, JOHN. "Before and After Roger Williams," <u>The Journal of Religious History</u>, 4 (Dec.), 1-13.
    Analysis of <u>The Bloudy Tenent</u> as an important document for understanding the religious toleration issue both before and after Roger Williams. Presents biography with an analysis of times. "In him, - [Williams] - liberality had been inextricable from his biblical apprehension of life. In those who came after him it became progressively extricated."

3   WARREN, AUSTIN. "Roger Williams," in <u>The New England Conscience</u>. Ann Arbor: University of Michigan Press, pp. 52-66.
    Contains a biography of Williams and general discussion of his Separatist position and debates with Quakers and John Cotton.

<u>1967 A BOOKS</u>

1   ERDMANN, KARL DIETRICH. <u>Roger Williams: das Abenteuer der Freiheit</u>. Kiel: F. Hirt.
    Sees American tradition derived more from Williams than from French Enlightenment. Freedom of conscience for Williams was only on a political basis. Maintains that Williams was eclectic. He used not only Calvin but Luther or anyone else who appealed to him.

2   MORGAN, EDMUND. <u>Roger Williams: The Church and the State</u>. New York: Harcourt Brace.
    Discussion of Williams's thoughts on the church and the state as presented in his writings. Focuses on five major areas in discussion of Williams: (1) the distinction between Puritan, Congregationalist, and Separatist, (2) the ministry, (3) the church and state in Massachusetts, (4) the basis of government, and (5) the business of government. What distinguished Williams as a church leader was his commitment to his conscience and the ability to follow through on his beliefs. Demonstrates how much of what Cotton and Winthrop believed was the same as what Williams believed. "In thinking about the church, Williams took a number of accepted doctrines and pressed them to unaccepted conclusions. The same is true about his thinking about the state." Reviewed in both <u>American Historical Review</u> and <u>Journal of American History</u> for June 1968.

1967

3   MUELLER, DONALD A. Song For A New World. Boston: Baker Plays.
    A musical in one act with Williams as a central hero of the democratic way of life.

4   POLISHOOK, IRWIN H., ed. Roger Williams, John Cotton, and Religious Freedom: A Controversy in Old and New England. Englewood Cliffs: Prentice Hall.
    Primarily a source study of the debate with large excerpts from The Bloudy Tenent and Cotton's replies to it. Detailed introduction outlines the issues in the debate and provides an historical background on Williams and his contemporaries in both England and New England.

5   REINITZ, RICHARD MARTIN. "Symbolism and Freedom: The Use of Biblical Typology As An Argument for Religious Toleration in Seventeenth Century England and America." Ph.D. dissertation. University of Rochester.
    Sees Williams's use of typology as developing out of the commitment to religious liberty "which in turn was based upon a peculiar conception of the nature of the conscience. He could not have arrived at such a commitment by the use of typology alone." Examines the background history of typology in Williams's day and earlier.

1967 B SHORTER WRITINGS

1   BERCOVITCH, SACVAN. "Typology in Puritan New England--The Williams-Cotton Controversy Reassessed," American Quarterly, 19 (Summer), 166-191.
    Disagrees with Miller's view on the question of typology as heresy being the central thesis in the debate with Cotton. "The controversy reveals not a clash between a typologist and a Puritan, but an opposition between two different typological approaches. It is an opposition which has behind it a long tradition...." The basic difference between Williams and Cotton was a difference over the allegorical and historical modes of typology. The typological argument of Williams is identified with Augustine while the ideas of Cotton are identified with Eusebius.

1968 A BOOKS

1   PETERSON, HELEN S. Roger Williams, A Colony Leader. Champaign: Garrard Publishing Co.
    Illustrated book about Williams's life for young children.

1968

2 WRIGHT, PAUL ORRIN. "Roger Williams: God's Swordsman in Searching Times." Ph.D. dissertation. Dallas Theological Seminary.
An exposition of the quality of "religious belief found in the writings of Roger Williams" and a demonstration of his conception of himself [Williams] as a prophet of the Lord defending the pure church against the antichrists of the seventeenth century." Sees three major influences on Williams: (1) the Protestant experience of the sixteenth and seventeenth centuries, (2) the Puritan experience in relation to church purity, and (3) his colonial experience as a representative of Rhode Island sent to England in the midst of civil war. Explains the symbol of the two-edged sword of Christ in Williams's writings and analyses the use of Scripture by him. Detailed explication of Williams's writings.

1968 B SHORTER WRITINGS

1 CONLEY, PATRICK. "Rhode Island Constitutional Development, 1636-1775," Rhode Island History, 27: 49-63.
Analyses Williams's role in various attempts at governing the colony of Rhode Island. Examines Williams's ideas on church and state and the relation of these ideas to his concept of typology. Importance of Williams's contributions to early history.

2 JOHNSTON, THOMAS E., Jr. "A Note on the Voices of Anne Bradstreet, Edward Taylor, Roger Williams, and Phillip Pain," Early American Literature, III (Fall), 125-126.
Discusses Williams's poetry in A Key and concludes that Williams's voice is Christian, and at times serious, dignified, admonitory, and authoritative. Also discusses the restrained, humble, and prayerful compassionate tone of Williams's poetic expression.

3 ROSENMEIER, JESPER. "The Teacher and the Witness: John Cotton and Roger Williams," William and Mary Quarterly, 3rd ser., 25 (July), 408-431.
Demonstrates that the main point of argument for each writer in the debate was the nature of Christ's incarnation and the ways in which both Cotton and Williams employed typology to interpret this. Williams's idea of Christ's incarnation was radically different in which Christ's kingdom became spiritual only. This is why Williams rejected Cotton's belief in the gradual redemption of man.

1969

1969 A BOOKS

1   CHUPACK, HENRY. <u>Roger Williams</u>. New York: Twayne Publishers.
    Basic introduction to Williams and his works organized along biographical lines. Examines the importance of the religious background of Williams's thought. Summarizes the important points about each of Williams's writings and explains the context within which they were written. Also includes extensive bibliography of primary and secondary items.

2   JOHNSTON, THOMAS E., Jr. "American Puritan Poetic Voices: Essays on Anne Bradstreet, Edward Taylor, Roger Williams, and Phillip Pain." Ph.D. dissertation. Ohio University.
    Discusses Williams's poetry in <u>A Key</u> and concludes that Williams's "voice" is Christian and at times, dignified, admonitory and authoritative. Also discusses the restrained, humble, and prayerful compassionate tone of Williams's poetic expression. <u>See</u> (1968.B2).

1969 B SHORTER WRITINGS

1   CAMP, LEON R. "Man and His Government: Roger Williams Vs. The Massachusetts Oligarchy," in <u>Preaching in American History, Selected Issues in the American Pulpit, 1630-1967</u>. Edited by Dewitte Holland. New York: Abingdon Press, pp. 74-97.
    Deals with the education and preaching of Williams in both England and America. Provides a useful discussion of the educational background of Williams and the issues involved in his banishment. Deals only with the period in Williams's life in Massachusetts prior to banishment.

2   MEAD, SIDNEY E. "Church, State, Calvinism, and Conscience," in <u>Perspectives in American History</u>, III: 443-459.
    An important review of Edmund Morgan's book, <u>Roger Williams, The Church and the State</u> (1967.A2), in which Mead elaborates on the point made by Morgan that Calvinism was at the center of Williams's thought.

3   SWAN, BRADFORD F. "New Light on Roger Williams and the Indians," <u>Providence Sunday Journal Magazine</u> (23 November), pp. 12-15.
    A newly discovered letter brings a closer view of Williams's parley with the Indians when Providence was burned during King Philip's War. The letter dated April 1, 1676 is a copy of one written by Williams to his brother Robert in Newport and warning of the Indians' deeds. <u>See also</u> (1971.B3).

Roger Williams: A Reference Guide

1970

1970 A BOOKS

1 GARRETT, JOHN. <u>Roger Williams: Witness Beyond Christendom, 1603-1683</u>. New York: Macmillan.

   Biography that devotes first chapter to Williams's life and the remaining chapters to a detailed discussion of the various aspects of Williams's life as revealed in his writings. Discusses the importance of the Bible and Calvinism in Williams's theology. Examines such subjects as Separatism, Seekerism, politics, the Quaker debates, and the relation of Williams and the people of Rhode Island. Demonstrates how Williams read the Bible and how important it is to understanding his ideas on church and state. Includes extensive background on English Separatists as well as selected bibliography on Williams.

2 HUNSAKER, ORVIL GLADE. "Calvinistic Election and Arminian Reparation: A Striking Contrast in the Works of Roger Williams and John Milton." Ph.D. dissertation, University of Illinois.

   Studies the difference between Milton and Williams on the subject of individual liberty. Examines the ideas of both writers on the subject of the divine role assigned to man's fallen nature, divine grace, the Book of Nature, the Book of Scripture, the idea of the 'called' writer, religious liberty, and civil liberty. Williams's position reflected the Calvinistic assurance that certain men had been predestined to salvation. Shows how Williams felt that religious and civil affairs were to accord with God's plan for regeneration.

1970 B SHORTER WRITINGS

1 CONLEY, PATRICK THOMAS. "Rhode Island Constitutional Development, 1636-1841: Prologue to the Dorr Rebellion." Ph.D. dissertation. University of Notre Dame. Chapters 1-2.

   Chapters 1 and 2 deal with Williams's role in setting up the charter and constitution of Rhode Island. Examines Williams's ideas on church and state and their relation to the early government of Providence. Shows how Williams's use of typology was important to role of leadership.

2 DAVIS, JACK L. "Roger Williams Among the Narragansett Indians," <u>New England Quarterly</u>, 43 (Dec.), 593-604.

   Argues that "Williams' intimate acquaintance with Narragansett culture provided the catalyst for both his powerful attack upon New England theocracy and his conception of an ideal commonwealth with which to supplant it."

1970

3   HINES, DONALD M. "Odd Customs and Strange Ways: The American Indian, c. 1640," Western Review, 7: 20-29.
    Examines the treatment of the Indian in Williams's A Key, that reveals "his sympathetic attitude and interest in such a people and their folkways," Williams's treatise is far more valuable than just an annal document as it has been treated.

4   REINITZ, RICHARD M. "The Typological Argument for Religious Toleration: The Separatist Tradition and Roger Williams," Early American Literature, V, i (Spring), 74-110.
    Demonstrates how Williams was following in the mainstream of a number of other writers who used biblical typology as a defense of religious toleration. Discusses the use of typology in the works of such writers as Henry Ainsworth, John Canne, and Robert Browne. The greatest influence upon Williams was the writing and thought of John Robertson, the spiritual leader at Plymouth with whom Williams was obviously acquainted. Explains how Williams used typological arguments in The Bloudy Tenent and other writings.

1971 A BOOKS

1   CHAPIN, HOWARD MILLAR, ed. "Introduction," A Key Into the Language of America. Ann Arbor: Gryphon Books.
    Reprint of 1936.B5 with same introduction.

2   SEARLES, JOAN CAROLYN. "The Worlds of Roger Williams." Ph.D. dissertation. Pennsylvania State University.
    The basic idea advanced here is that Williams's writings and the literary qualities of them have been neglected and that to understand the structure, tone, and meaning of Williams as a writer one must examine the writings closely. Focuses on four areas of investigation: the Indian world represented by A Key Into the Language of America, the world of Puritan controversy represented by Queries, The Bloudy Tenent, and Cotton's Letter Examined and Answered, the spiritual world represented by Experiments of Spiritual Life and Health, and finally, the world of the Quakers represented by George Fox Digg'd out of His Burrowes. Shows Williams's use of metaphor, thematic development, rhetorical skills, and development of tone in each of these areas.

3   SWAN, BRADFORD F. A Copy of A Letter of Roger Williams Telling of the Burning of Providence and of His Conference with the Indians During King Philip's War in 1676. Providence: Society of Colonial Wars.

Text of letter referred to in 1969.B3. Introduction and notes by Swan provide background information to substantiate the authenticity of the letter.

1971 B SHORTER WRITINGS

1   BOZEMAN, THEODORE D. "Religious Liberty and the Problem of Order in Early Rhode Island," <u>New England Quarterly</u>, 45, i (March), 44-64.

  Demonstrates how Williams believed in civil order and how he dealt with the problems in governing Rhode Island Discusses the different incidents that happened during Williams's period of leadership.

1972 A BOOKS

1   DIEMER, CARL J., Jr. "A Historical Study of Roger Williams in the Light of The Quaker Controversy." Ph.D. dissertation. Southwestern Baptist Theological Seminary.

  An extensive examination of Williams's role in the debates with the Quakers in 1672. This study attempts to show that in a critical test of his basic position on religious liberty, Williams did not compromise his basic ideas. Concludes that Williams was primarily a minister first and a politician only when necessary. "Williams showed a remarkable awareness of the weaknesses in Quaker theology in seventeenth-century New England. He detected that their dependence on the immediate inspiration of the Spirit was the primary difference between Quaker and Puritan theology, which relied on the Scriptures."

2   SKAGGS, DONALD K. "Roger Williams in History: His Image in the American Mind." Ph.D. dissertation. University of Southern California.

  Distinguishes between the real Williams and the various treatments of him by historians from Cotton Mather to Perry Miller. Offers an analysis of Williams's accomplishments and shortcomings. Concludes that although Williams has been greatly overestimated on the one hand and slandered on the other, his contributions to America are significant.

1972 B SHORTER WRITINGS

1   AUBIN, GEORGE F. "A Historical Phonology of Narragansett." Ph.D. dissertation. Brown University.

  Examines the evidence presented in Williams's <u>A Key</u> as a

Roger Williams: A Reference Guide

1972

(AUBIN, GEORGE F.)
means of reconstructing a phonology or system of sounds connected with the Narragansett language. Analysis is very specialized but ultimately based on Williams's observations about the vocabulary of the Narragansetts.

2 REINITZ, RICHARD M. "The Separatist Background of Roger Williams' Argument for Religious Toleration," in Typology and Early American Literature. Edited by Sacvan Bercovitch. Amherst: University of Massachusetts Press, pp. 107-137.
Discusses Williams's use of biblical typology as a defense of religious toleration. See 1970.B4.

1973 A BOOKS

1 TEUNISSEN, JOHN J. and EVELYN J. HINZ, eds. A Key Into the Language of America. Detroit: Wayne State University Press.
Detailed introduction, notes, and text of Williams's work. Introduction argues for the Key as one of the first examples of early American literature. "A Key is primarily an emblematic and sympathetic presentation of Indian life and an ironic and critical comment upon European civilization in general and New England in particular." Explanation of the theme of the Fall inherent in the entire work and the three part division of vocabulary, observations, and poems in each chapter of A Key. Includes literary history of A Key and selected bibliography of Williams scholarship.

1973 B SHORTER WRITINGS

1 REED, JOHN WILLIAM. "Church and State in Massachusetts, 1630-1660," in America in Controversy, History of American Public Address. Edited by Dewitte Holland. Dubuque: William C. Brown Company, pp. 19-34.
Offers a concise summary and analysis of the issues at stake in the Williams-Cotton controversy. Presents background of the debate in England and outlines the arguments of both Cotton and Williams on the church and the state and the relationship between the two. Includes lengthy excerpts from The Bloudy Tenent as well as Cotton's replies. Suggests the importance of the controversy not only to Puritan New England but for the later development of the church-state issue in America.

1974

2 _____. "Puritan Paternalism and Indian Evangelism, 1620-1675," in America in Controversy, History of American Public Address. Edited by Dewitte Holland. Dubuque: William C. Brown Company, pp. 1-18.

Examines Williams's work with the Indians. Shows how Williams considered that conversion of the Indians could not take place until they had first been civilized. Discusses Williams's ideas about ownership of the colonial lands by the Indians and the central importance of A Key Into the Language of America in the debate over Indian rights. Concludes that although Williams is alleged to have made many converts, his work with the Indians was primarily as peacemaker and friend.

3 TEUNISSEN, JOHN J. and EVELYN J. HINZ. "Roger Williams, St. Paul, and American Primitivism," The Canadian Review of American Studies, IV, ii (Fall), 121-136.

Analysis of the numerous references in Williams's writings to Saint Paul "With a view to suggesting that his relationship to the Apostle, as he conceived it, is best described as an archetypal one and that it is Williams's conception of himself as a Pauline figure which explains the particular character of his primitivism, indeed which allows him as a seventeenth-century Puritan to be a primitivist." Relates Williams's primitivism with his Calvinism.

4 ZIFF, LARZER. Puritanism in America: New Culture in a New World. New York: Viking Press, pp. 100-117.

Discusses three important aspects of Williams: (1) Williams's own self proclaimed role, (2) the controversy between Williams and John Cotton, (3) Williams's writing abilities. Discusses the important distinction between the political and religious side of Williams and its relation to the later life of Williams. Concludes with examination of Williams's writings by saying: "...in letters and expository works he pursued a humane diction and syntax in keeping with his perception that learning was now freed for application to the secular aims of men."

1974 A BOOKS

1 COYLE, EDWARD WALLACE. "From Sinner to Saint: A Study of the Critical Reputation of Roger Williams With An Annotated Bibliography of Writings About Him." Ph.D. dissertation. University of Massachusetts.

Examines the critical reactions to Williams from the seventeenth to the twentieth centuries. Demonstrates how

1974

    (COYLE, EDWARD WALLACE)
       the earliest reactions of the seventeenth and eighteenth centuries were largely negative. Nineteenth- and twentieth-century writers have examined Williams's thoughts and writings with a greater degree of objectivity and depth. Includes an annotated bibliography of all books, articles, dissertations, and master's theses written about Williams.

<u>1974 B SHORTER WRITINGS - NONE</u>

Author Index

Adelman, David C., 1955.B1
Adlam, Samuel, 1850.A1
Allen, R. W., 1852.B1
Allen, W. F., 1891.B1
Allen, Zachariah, 1860.A1
Ames, Charles Gordon, 1900.B1
Andrews, Charles M., 1936.B1
Anthony, Bertha Williams, 1949.A1; 1966.A1
Anthony, Henry B., 1875.B1
Aptheker, Herbert, 1966. B1
Armitage, Thomas, 1887.B1
Arnold, Fred A., 1895.B1
Arnold, Samuel Green, 1859.A1; 1864.B1
Atkins, Clyde W., 1936.B3
Aspinwall, Thomas, 1862.B1
Aubin, George F., 1972.B1
Austin, John, 1889.B1; 1897.A1, 1897.A2

Bach, Marcus, 1940.A1
Backus, Isaac, 1777.B1
Bainton, Roland H., 1951.B1
Bancroft, George, 1843.B1
Banning, H. E., 1890.B1
Barker, Arthur, 1942.B1
Barker, Shirley, 1965.B1
Barrows, C. E., 1876.B1
Barry, John, 1855.B1
Bartlett, John R., 1864.B2; 1866.A1; 1882.B1
Bell, J. D., 1857.B1
Belmont, Perry, 1927.B1
Benedict, David, 1813.B1
Bercovitch, Sacvan, 1967.B1

Bicknell, Thomas, 1918.A1, 1918.B2
Bondy, Joseph, 1927.A1
Bozeman, Theodore, 1971.B1
Bradford, William, 1647.B1
Bradley, C. S., 1871.B1
Brasch, Fred E., 1931.B1
Brigham, C. S., 1900.B2; 1902.B2
Brockunier, Samuel H., 1937.A1; 1939.B1; 1940.A2
Bronson, B. F., 1872.B1
Brooks, Mrs. Henry, 1896.B1
Browne, Benjamin, 1961.B1
Burke, William, 1757.B1
Burlingame, Roger, 1956.B1
Burrage, Henry S., 1879.B1; 1880.B1; 1899.B1; 1901.B1
Butterworth, Hezekiah, 1897.A3

Calamandrei, Mauro, 1952.B1; 1953.A1
Caldwell, Samuel, 1866.A2; 1872.B2
Callender, John, 1739.B1
Camp, Leon, 1963.B1; 1964.B1; 1969.B1
Campbell, Douglas, 1892.B1
Carmer, Carl, 1956.B2
Carpenter, Edmund J., 1902.B3; 1908.B1; 1909.A1
Chalmers, George, 1780.B1
Chancellor, Frank, 1936.B5
Chapin, Howard Millar, 1916.A1; 1918.A2, 1918.A3, 1918.B3; 1923.B1; 1924.A1; 1928.A1, 1928.B2; 1934.A1; 1936.A1; 1971.A1

Child, Mrs. Anne P., 1866.A3
Christian, John T., 1922.B1; 1926.B1
Chupack, Henry, 1969.A1
Clarke, J. C. C., 1876.B2
Cleal, C. H., 1955.B2
Colcord, W. A., 1907.B1
Conley, Patrick, 1968.B1; 1970.B1
Cotton, John, 1643.A1; 1647.A1
Covey, Cyclone, 1966.A2
Cowell, Henry J., 1924.B1
Coyle, Edward Wallace, 1974.A1
Creel, George, 1921.B2
Crichton, Robert J., 1961.A1

Davis, David, 1932.B1
Davis, Jack L., 1970.B2
Dawson, Joseph, 1955.B3; 1956.B3
Dean, J. W., 1896.B2
Deane, Charles, 1873.B1; 1884.B1
Denison, Frederic, 1872.A1
Denison, Merrill, 1939.A1
Dexter, Henry Martyn, 1875.B2; 1876.A1; 1879.B2; 1881.A1
Diemer, Carl J., 1972.A1
Diman, J. Lewis, 1866.A4; 1877.A1
Dorr, Henry C., 1882.B2; 1885.B1; 1895.B2
Dos Passos, John, 1941.B1
Douglas, William, 1747.B1
Drowne, Henry Russell, 1910.B1
Durfee, Job, 1832.A1
Durfee, Thomas, 1886.B1
Duyckinck, Evert A. and George L., 1875.B3

Eager, George B., 1920.B1
Eales, Henry S., 1936.B5
Eames, B. T., 1872.B3
Easton, Emily, 1930.A1; 1936.B6
Eaton, Amasa, 1908.A1
Eaton, Jeanette, 1944.A1
Eddy, D. C., 1861.A1
Edwards, Cecile Pepin, 1957.A1
Edwards, Morgan, 1867.B1
Eggleston, Edward, 1896.B3; 1897.B1
Elliott, Charles W., 1857.B2
Ellis, George E., 1891.B2

Elton, Romeo, 1853.A1
Ely, W. D., 1892.A1; 1894.B2
Emerson, Everett, 1965.B2
Erdmann, Karl Dietrich, 1967.A1
Ernst, James, 1928.A2; 1929.A1, 1929.B2; 1931.B2; 1932.A1; 1935.B2
Evans, John, 1819.B1

Faunce, W. H. Perry, 1903.B1
Felt, Joseph, 1855.B2
Fiske, John, 1898.B1; 1899.B2
Foord, John, 1876.B3
Ford, Worthington C., 1647.B1
Foster, John, 1838.B1
Fox, George, 1678.A1
Freund, Michael, 1927.B2; 1933.B1

Gallup, Clarence M., 1930.A2; 1935.A1
Gammell, William, 1845.A1
Gannon, Freda, 1961.A2
Gardiner, George, 1936.A2
Garrett, John, 1966.B2; 1970.A1
Gaustad, Edwin S., 1958.B1
Gervinus, G. G., 1853.B1
Goodwin, J. A., 1888.B2
Graves, J. R., 1858.B1
Greene, George W., 1877.B1
Greene, Theodore P., 1964.A1
Grose, Howard B., 1936.B7
Grosvenor, Cyrus Pitt, 1847.B1
Guild, Reuben Aldridge, 1862.A2; 1866.A5, 1866.A6; 1886.A2; 1887.A1, 1887.B2; 1892.A2
Gummere, Richard M., 1958.B2; 1963.B2

Haley, J. W., 1928.A3
Hall, May Emery, 1917.A1
Hall, Ruth, 1901.A1
Haller, William, 1934.B2; 1955.B4
Ham, Mason, 1930.B1
Harkness, R. E. E., 1935.B3; 1936.B8
Harris, Hugh, 1944.B1
Hildreth, Richard, 1877.B2
Hines, Donald M., 1970.B3

Index

Hinman, Royal Ralph, 1838.B2
Hinz, Evelyn J., 1973.A1
Hirsch, Elizabeth Feist, 1941.B2
Hodges, Almon Danforth, 1899.B3; 1900.B3
Holman, Winnifred L., 1952.B2
Hopkins, Stephen, 1771.B1
Hosmer, James K., 1908.B2
Howland, John Andrews, 1886.B2
Hubbard, William, 1680.B1
Hudson, Winthrop, 1951.A1, 1951.B2; 1953.B1; 1964.B2
Hunsaker, Orvil Glade, 1970.A2
Hutchinson, Thomas, 1764.B1

Isham, Norman M., 1925.B1
Ives, J. Moss, 1931.B3

Jantz, Harold, 1962.B1
Johnson, Albert, 1957.A2
Johnson, Edward, 1653.B1
Johnson, Lorenzo, 1839.A1
Johnson, Lucian, 1903.B2
Johnston, Thomas E., Jr., 1968.B2; 1969.A2
Jordan, Winthrop K., 1938.B1

Kimball, G. S., 1912.B1
King, Henry Melville, 1880.A1; 1896.A1; 1897.A4; 1903.B3; 1907.A1; 1908.B3; 1909.A2, 1909.B1; 1917.A1
Knowles, James D., 1834.A1
Kohler, Max J., 1903.B4

Leighton, Etta V., 1912.A1
Lewis, Myrtle M., 1935.B3
Lodge, Henry C., 1877.B4
Longacre, Charles S., 1939.A2
Lowenherz, Robert J., 1959.B1
Lowndes, G. A., 1889.B2

Mackie, J. M., 1845.B1
M'Carty, Rev. J. H., 1866.B1
McDougall, Frances, 1860.A2
Massachusetts House Bill, 1936.B9

Masson, David, 1859.B1
Mather, Cotton, 1702.B1
Matthews, Albert R., 1900.B4
Mead, Sidney E., 1969.B2
Mecklin, John M., 1934.B3
Merriman, Titus M., 1892.A3; 1903.B5
Miller, Charles T., 1874.A1
Miller, Perry, 1935.B5; 1953.A2; 1963.B3
Moehlman, Conrad Henry, 1934.B4
Moore, John, 1950.B1
Moore, Leroy, Jr., 1963.B4; 1965.B3, 1965.B4
Moreland, Marc, 1945.B1
Morgan, Edmund S., 1965.B5; 1967.A2
Moriarity, G. A., Jr., 1913.B1
Morison, Samuel Eliot, 1952.B3
Morris, Charles, 1919.B1
Morris, Maxwell H., 1951.B3
Morris, Richard B., 1921.B3
Morton, Nathaniel, 1669.B1
Mowry, William A., 1909.A3
Mudge, Rev. Z. A., 1871.A1
Mueller, David L., 1958.B3
Mueller, Donald A., 1967.A3

Neal, Daniel, 1747.B2
Newman, A. H., 1892.B2; 1894.B3
Newman, Louis Israel, 1942.B2
Niebuhr, Richard, 1956.B4
Noyes, Isaac P., 1886.B3; 1907.A2
Nygaard, Norman E., 1964.B2

Osgood, Herbert L., 1904.B1

Page, Samuel Davis, 1916.B1
Paine, George T., 1896.A2
Palfrey, John G., 1858.B2
Parkes, Henry Bamford, 1931.B4
Parkman, F., 1834.B1
Parrington, Vernon L., 1927.B3
Payne, Earnest, 1961.A2
Pearson, Milo E., 1930.B2
Peattie, Donald C., 1946.B1; 1949.B1
Perley, Sidney, 1916.B2

Peterson, Frank, 1920.B2
Peterson, Helen, 1968.A1
Piercy, Josephine, 1938.B2
Polishook, Irwin H., 1967.A4
Poteat, Edwin M., 1940.A3
Potter, George R., 1920.B3
Purnell, T. R., 1867.B2

Rae, W. F., 1881.B1; 1882.B3
Ramsay, David, 1818.B1
Reed, John William, 1966.A3; 1973.B1, 1973.B2
Rees, Gilbert, 1950.A1
Reinitz, Richard Martin, 1967.A5; 1970.B4; 1972.B2
Richardson, Erastus, 1889.A1
Richman, Irving B., 1908.A2
Rider, Sidney S., 1862.A1; 1886.B4; 1888.B3; 1891.A1, 1891.B3; 1894.B4; 1896.A3, 1896.B4; 1897.A5; 1904.B2, 1904.B3; 1912.B2
Robertson, William, 1777.B2
Roddy, Clarence S., 1948.A1, 1948.B1
Rosenmeier, Jasper, 1965.B6; 1968.B3
Rossiter, Clinton L., 1951.B4; 1953.B2
Russell, William, 1778.B1
Rusterholtz, Wallace P., 1938.B3
L. A. R., 1878.B1

Savelle, Max, 1942.B3
Savage, James, 1649.B1
Schevill, James, 1957.A3
Schneider, Herbert W., 1930.B3
Schultz, Harold J., 1962.B2
Scott, M. B., 1869.B1
Seager, Allan, 1939.B2
Seccombe, T., 1900.B5
Searles, Joan Carolyn, 1971.A2
Seymour, C. C. B., 1858.B3
Shaaf, David S., 1936.B10
Sherman, David, 1860.B1
Simon, Abram, 1912.A2
Simpson, Alan, 1956.B5
Skaggs, Donald K., 1972.A2
Stead, George Albert, 1934.B5

Stewart, Walter Sinclair, 1925.B2
Stone, Thomas T., 1872.A2
Straus, Oscar, 1893.B1; 1894.A1; 1919.A2; 1926.B2
Straus, Roger Williams, 1936.A3
Strickland, Arthur B., 1919.A1
Swan, Bradford, 1942.B4; 1944.A2, 1944.B2; 1946.B2; 1949.B1; 1969.B3; 1971.A3
Sweet, William Warren, 1942.B5

Terris, Walter Franklin, 1962.B3
Teunissen, John J. and Evelyn J. Hinz, 1973.A1, 1973.B3
Thompson, Luther Joe, 1952.A1
Tilley, Winthrop, 1932.B2
Tooker, William Wallace, 1894.B5, 1894.B6
Trumbull, Annie Eliot, 1900.A1
Trumbull, Benjamin, 1810.B1
Trumbull, J. Hammond, 1866.A7
Tuckerman, Henry T., 1857.B3
Tyler, Moses Coit, 1878.B2

Underhill, Edward Bean, 1846.A1; 1851.B1
United States Congress, 1872.B4
Upham, W. P., 1866.B2; 1870.B1

Vaughn, Alden T., 1965.B7
Vose, James G., 1894.B7

Walker, W., 1894.B8
Wall, Caleb A., 1888.B4
Ward, Nathaniel, 1647.B2
Warren, Austin, 1966.B3
Waters, Henry F., 1889.B3; 1893.B2
Wayland, Francis, 1860.B3
Weiner, Frederick B., 1935.B6
Whipple, Francis H., 1843.B2
White, Elizabeth Nicholson, 1957.A4
Whitsett, William H., 1896.A4
Willison, George F., 1945.B2
Winslow, Ola Elizabeth, 1957.A5, 1957.B1
Winsor, Justin, 1881.B2

Index

Winthrop, John, 1649.B2, 1649.B3
Withers, Richard E., 1966.B4
Wood, William, 1634.B1
Woodward, Carl R., 1957.B2
Wright, Paul Orrin, 1968.A2

Wroth, Lawrence, 1936.B11, 1937.A2

Z. Z. Z., 1839.B1
Ziff, Larzer, 1962.B4; 1973.B4

Selected Subject and Title Index

Apple Tree Root and, 1861.B1
As To Roger Williams and His
    Banishment, 1876.A1; 1879.B1;
    1880.B1

Banishment of, 1649.B1, 1649.B2;
    1838.B2; 1858.B2; 1875.B2;
    1876.A1; 1884.B1; 1886.B1;
    1891.B2; 1892.A3; 1894.B3;
    1901.B1
Baptism of, 1777.B1; 1813.B1;
    1861.A1; 1867.B1; 1880.A1;
    1887.B1; 1894.B2
Baptists and, 1771.B1; 1813.B1;
    1861.A1; 1867.B1; 1880.A1;
    1887.B1; 1894.B2; 1896.A2;
    1897.A4; 1907.A1; 1922.B1;
    1925.B2; 1926.B1; 1940.A3;
    1955.B2; 1961.B1; 1965.B3
Barnard, Mary (maiden name of
    wife), 1886.B4; 1899.B3;
    1900.B2, 1900.B3; 1936.B6;
    1957.A4
Bible and, 1942.B2; 1948.A1,
    1948.B1, 1967.A2; 1968.A2;
    1970.A2
Bibliography of, 1881.B2; 1902.B2;
    1972.A2; 1974.A1
Biography, 1819.B1; 1834.A1;
    1839.A1; 1843.B1; 1845.A1;
    1853.A1; 1866.A5; 1871.A1;
    1887.A1; 1894.A2; 1896.B2;
    1900.B5; 1908.B1; 1909.A1;
    1917.A1; 1919.A1, 1919.A2;
    1923.B1; 1930.A1; 1939.A2;
    1940.A2; 1957.A1, 1957.A5;
    1961.A3; 1964.A2; 1969.A1;
    1970.A1

Birth of, 1840.B1; 1887.A1
Bloudy Tenent, 1846.A1; 1866.A2;
    1875.B3; 1878.B1; 1971.A2
Bloudy Tenent Yet More Bloudy,
    1875.B3; 1878.B1; 1971.A2
Boston, 1634.B1; 1643.A1;
    1647.B1; 1649.B1, 1649.B3
Bradford, William, 1647.B1;
    1649.B1, 1649.B2
Burial of, 1918.A2; 1934.B1

Calvin, 1909.B1; 1920.B1; 1969.B2
Calvinistic Election, 1952.A1;
    1968.A2; 1970.A2
Cambridge, 1936.B5
Children of, 1881.A1; 1889.B1
Christenings make Not Christians,
    1881.A1; 1971.A2
Civil War In England, 1900.B4;
    1927.B2; 1931.B2; 1933.B1;
    1942.B1
Classics, 1958.B2; 1963.B2
Compass of, 1902.B1; 1936.B2
Complete Writings of Roger Williams,
    The, 1963.B3; 1965.B5
Contributions of, 1935.B3, 1935.B6;
    1936.B8; 1939.B2; 1945.B1;
    1953.B2
Cotton, John, 1893.B1; 1931.B4;
    1941.B2; 1955.B4; 1962.B4;
    1965.B2, 1965.B6; 1966.A3;
    1967.B4; 1968.B3; 1973.B1

Death of, 1918.A2; 1934.B1
Declaration of Independence and
    1955.B3, 1956.B3; 1956.B5;
    1964.B2; 1965.B4

Democracy and, 1939.B1; 1952.B1;
    1953.B2; 1955.B3; 1956.B3,
    1956.B5; 1964.B2
Descendents of, 1886.A1; 1889.B1,
    1889.B2; 1893.B2; 1912.B2;
    1913.B1; 1935.B4

Early Baptists Defended, 1880.A1
Education of, 1966.A2; 1968.A2
Eliot, John and, 1892.B2; 1917.A2
England, 1929.B2; 1942.B1
The Examiner-Defended in a Fair
    and Sober Answer, 1971.A2
Experiments of Spiritual Life and
    Health, 1862.A1; 1951.A1;
    1971.A2

Fictional Works About, 1832.A1;
    1860.A2; 1866.A1; 1872.A1;
    1900.A1; 1901.A1; 1907.A2;
    1930.A2; 1935.A1; 1939.A1;
    1940.A1; 1944.A1; 1950.A1;
    1957.A1, 1957.A2, 1957.A3
Forgeries Connected With, 1896.A1,
    1896.A2
Fourth Paper Presented by Major
    Butler, 1963.B3
Fox, George and, 1678.A1; 1866.A4;
    1924.B1

Gentle Radical, The, 1966.A3;
    1933.B1
Genealogy of, 1886.A1; 1889.B1,
    1889.B3; 1893.B2; 1912.B2;
    1913.B1; 1929.B1; 1935.B4;
    1949.A1; 1952.B2
George Fox Digg'd out of His
    Burrowes, 1866.A4; 1971.A2
Grave of, 1918.A2; 1934.B1

Harris, William and, 1896.A2,
    1896.A3
The Hireling Ministry None of
    Christs, 1971.A2
Historians and, 1963.B4; 1964.A1;
    1972.A2
"How Democratic Was Roger
    Williams?" 1965.B5

Insane and, 1946.B2
Indians and, 1892.A2; 1894.B6;
    1895.B2; 1896.A3, 1896.A4;
    1936.A2; 1965.B3; 1969.B3;
    1970.B3; 1973.A1, 1973.B2
The Irrepressible Democrat, Roger
    Williams, 1940.A2

Jefferson, Thomas and, 1955.B3;
    1956.B3
Jews and, 1903.B3; 1912.A2;
    1921.B3; 1951.B3; 1955.B1

A Key Into the Language of America,
    1794.B1; 1827.B1; 1833.B1;
    1866.A7; 1892.A1; 1894.B1,
    1894.B4; 1894.B5; 1936.B11,
    1937.A2; 1938.B2; 1949.B2;
    1962.B1; 1968.B2; 1970.B3;
    1971.A1; 1973.A1, 1973.B2
King's Colors, Roger Williams and,
    1928.A2, 1928.B2

Leadership of, 1944.A2; 1966.B4
Letters of Roger Williams,
    1866.A1; 1882.B1; 1889.B2;
    1924.A1; 1944.B2; 1971.A3
Linguistics and, 1972.B1
London and, 1944.B1

Magnalia Christi Americana,
    1702.B1
Marriage of, 1886.B4; 1899.B3;
    1900.B3; 1918.B1; 1936.B6
Massachusetts, 1764.B1; 1855.B1;
    1873.B1; 1887.B2; 1934.B5
Massachusetts Historical Society
    edition of A Key, 1794.B1
Master Roger Williams, 1957.A3
Memoir of Roger Williams, 1834.A1
Milton, John and, 1859.B1;
    1920.B3; 1970.A2
Monuments to, 1860.B2; 1872.B3,
    1872.B4; 1875.B1; 1877.A1;
    1895.B1; 1921.B1
Mr. Cotton's Letter Examined and
    Answered, 1866.A6

Index

Narragansett Indians and, 1885.B1; 1892.A2; 1965.B7
"Neglected Aspects of Roger Williams' Thought," 1952.B1
New England Firebrand Quenched, 1678.A1

Of Plymouth Plantation, 1647.B1; 1952.B3
Pilgrims, 1647.B1; 1908.B3
Pilgrims, Puritans, and Roger Williams Vindicated, 1892.A3
Plymouth and, 1864.B1; 1871.B1; 1942.B4
Poetry of, 1968.B2; 1971.A2
Political Thought of Roger Williams, The, 1928.A1; 1929.A1
Portraits of, 1891.A1
Preaching of, 1966.A2; 1973.B1
Primitivism, 1973.B3
Providence, Settlement of, 1859.A1; 1864.B1; 1912.B1
Providence, Letter to Town of, 1942.B2
Puritan Revolution and, 1900.B4; 1927.B2; 1931.B2; 1933.B1; 1942.B1

Quakers and, 1959.B1; 1963.B1; 1972.A1
Quaker Debates of 1672, 1959.B1; 1963.B1; 1972.A1
Queries of Highest Consideration, 1971.A2

"Religious Thought of Roger Williams, The," 1948.A1, 1948.B1
Reputation of, 1963.B4; 1964.A1; 1972.A2; 1974.A1
Rhode Island Historical Society Manuscripts, 1949.B3
Rise of Puritansim, The, 1934.B2
"Roger Williams: An Essay in Interpretation," 1963.B3
Roger Williams: The Church and the State, 1967.A2

"Roger Williams: His Image in the American Mind," 1972.A2
Roger Williams, New England Firebrand, 1932.A1
"Roger Williams, Seeker," 1927.B3
Roger Williams: His Contribution to the American Tradition, 1953.A2
Roger Williams; Witness Beyond Christendom, 1603-1683, 1970.A1
Roger Williams and the Massachusetts Magistrates, 1964.A1
Royal Society and, 1931.B1; 1932.B2

Saint Paul, 1973.B3
Saints and Strangers, 1945.B
Salem and the House of, 1866.B2; 1870.B1; 1888.B1; 1896.B1; 1916.B2; 1930.B2
Seals of, 1935.B2
Seeker, 1927.B3; 1928.B1
Soul Liberty and, 1897.A5; 1903.B1
State and Church relations, 1940.A2; 1967.A2
Statues of, 1872.B3; 1895.B1
Sundial of, 1936.B2

Toleration and, 1857.B3
Trading post of, 1934.A1
Typology and, 1953.A2; 1967.B1; 1967.A5; 1970.B4; 1972.B2

Urquhart, Sir Thomas and, 1900.B4

Vane, Sir Henry, Jr. and, 1909.A2

Watch of, 1910.B1
Williams, James, 1889.B3
Williams, Mary (wife). See Barnard, Mary
Winthrop, John, 1649.B1, 1649.B2
"World of Roger Williams, The," 1971.A2

Writings of Roger Williams, The, 1866.A1, 1866.A2
Writings of (group), 1862.A2; 1872.B2; 1875.B3; 1878.B1; 1918.A3, 1918.B1; 1969.A1
Wroth, Lawrence, 1936.B11; 1937.A2